Getting

Second Edition

Also available from Continuum
Guerilla Guide to Teaching 2nd Edition – Sue Cowley
Getting the Buggers to Behave 3rd Edition – Sue Cowley
Getting the Buggers to Write – Sue Cowley
How to Survive Your First Year in Teaching – Sue Cowley
Letting the Buggers Be Creative – Sue Cowley
100 Ideas for Teaching Thinking Skills – Stephen Bowkett
Sue Cowley's Teaching Clinic – Sue Cowley
Sue Cowley's A–Z of Teaching – Sue Cowley
Teaching Thinking – Robert Fisher

Getting the Buggers to Think

SECOND EDITION

SUE COWLEY

continuum

Continuum International Publishing Group
The Tower Building   80 Maiden Lane, Suite 704
11 York Road   New York, NY 10038
London SE1 7NX

www.continuumbooks.com

© Sue Cowley 2007

British Library Cataloguing-in-Publication Data
A catalogue record for this book is available from the British Library.

ISBN: 0–8264–9281–9 (paperback)
      978–08264–9281–4 (paperback)

Library of Congress Cataloging-in-Publication Data
A catalog record for this book is available from the Library of Congress.

Typeset by Servis Filmsetting Ltd, Manchester
Printed and bound in Great Britain by Ashford Colour Press, Gosport, Hampshire.

With special thanks to the girls:
Elka, Véronique, Lucy, Mandi, Penny and Mélanie

Contents

Acknowledgements

Many thanks to everyone at my publishers, Continuum, especially to Anthony Haynes for the original 'Buggers' title, which really started the ball rolling. A huge 'thank you' to Alexandra Webster for all her hard work as my editor, to Suzanne Ashley and Katie Sayers for marketing input, and to Christina Garbutt for all the admin and other stuff.

A special 'thank you' goes to the two people without whom it just wouldn't happen – Tilak and Álvie, my wonderful boys.

Introduction

Learning how to think is, surely, what education is all about. As teachers, we have the crucial task of helping our children understand how to think effectively, and showing them how they can best use their amazing brains. With quality approaches to the teaching of thinking skills, learning becomes a wonderful and thrilling experience for our students; one that can and should last a lifetime. Rather than being a boring prison that they cannot wait to escape, school turns into a place where our children are inspired, where we light the flame of a lifelong passion for learning.

Some people would have us believe that school is about learning facts and figures, techniques and skills, things that can be tested and measured so that we know who is clever and who is the 'best'. This approach also offers a way for the powers that be to test us as teachers, to find out who is adding the most 'value' to their students (as though children were some kind of supermarket product). When it comes down to it, though, without the ability to use our brains in an inventive and imaginative way, we would be little more than robots, swallowing information and learning skills, but unable to actually apply them to real-life situations.

Learning how to think, and to think properly, is a very exciting process. There is a real sense of wonder when children realize just how imaginative they are, or how many new ideas and approaches they can dream up, or how they can apply logic to make sense of a situation. Teaching our children how to think also means showing them the techniques involved in high-quality thinking, such as learning how to think in a structured way, or the little tricks of the trade that can help us remember.

At an early age I realized that I could use my brain in a way that would help make me appear 'clever'. For instance, I made up little tricks that helped me remember my spellings. As teachers, we can pass on these techniques to our own children, opening up the door to effective thinking, and helping them to develop their true potential. You'll find lots of these methods described in this book, along with plenty of ideas for activities and exercises that you can use within your lessons to develop your students' thinking.

For those children who struggle academically, school can be a confusing and even fearful place. They have huge quantities of information thrown at them but they have little hope of actually retaining much of it. They are expected to write essays, to work out sums, to carry out scientific experiments, without much idea of how to actually go about it. This leads, at least in part, to the disaffection and alienation that make both their lives and ours so miserable in the classroom; but once we open up the world of thinking to them, and show them how powerful and remarkable their brains truly are, we can re-engage them with the whole process of learning.

It seems increasingly that creativity is being crowded out of the curriculum at the moment. A climate that values only what can be tested is bound to leave little space for children to explore their world in an imaginative way. It is therefore doubly important that we make time to include activities that encourage the creative side of our students' minds. In the arena of thinking skills we can find so much to stretch and challenge the imagination. It is my hope that you will find lots of inspiration in this book to help you unlock the creative potential of your classes.

Teachers are so overloaded these days that it is tempting to believe there is simply no time for the teaching of thinking skills. You might feel such a strong pressure to work through the curriculum that you just can't see how you can fit in an additional area of learning. Fortunately, in many instances it is possible (and indeed best) to integrate the teaching of thinking skills directly into the subjects that you have to deliver. In addition, if we can develop better thinking skills in our students then they will have the tools they need to gain access to all areas of the curriculum.

This will often mean that we do not actually have to teach them by rote all the areas that are meant to be covered.

One of the biggest problems for teachers when approaching thinking skills is that this is an invisible area of learning. We can't tell just by looking whether or not our students are actually thinking. Is that distant look in their eyes an indication that they are deep in thought, and if they are, exactly what are they thinking about? Are they thinking about the work that we've set, or could it be that they are thinking about what they might have for lunch? Alternatively, is that glazed appearance simply a sign that they have turned off, and are not thinking at all – how on earth can we as teachers tell? You'll find plenty of ideas here about how to make your students' thinking processes more explicit and also lots of advice about using discussion activities to think in groups and as a whole class.

Traditionally, the teaching of thinking in schools has been connected closely with the teaching of philosophy or religious ideas. However, thinking is also about taking new approaches to problems, finding original solutions, solving mysteries, interpreting great works of art, and so on. Thinking can be very exciting and highly motivating for our students. What child doesn't love to solve puzzles, to look for clues in a murder mystery, to find strange and wacky new inventions? Thinking is great at levelling the playing field – you don't have to be academically able, or even all that experienced in life, to be able to think. When it comes to thought, and especially original thought, an eight-year-old child may have ideas that are as 'good' (and indeed often better) than those of a middle-aged adult.

Within this book you'll find lots of different information, ideas and approaches to help you develop your students' thinking skills. As with all my books, my aim here is to give you practical strategies for developing these skills, ones that you can actually put directly into use in your classroom. As well as offering you suggestions for exercises and activities, I also cover the organizational aspects of teaching thinking in a classroom setting. The advice that I give is applicable to teachers right across the primary and secondary spectrum and to those who are working in all areas of the curriculum. However, with so much to cram in, I hope you will understand that there is a limit to the amount of detail that I can offer in any one subject or Key Stage.

I'd like to end this introduction by wishing you all the best of luck in developing thinking in your own classroom. Just think what joy it will bring you if you can be at least partially responsible for lighting the flame of a love for learning within your children – a light that will never fade.

Sue Cowley
www.suecowley.co.uk

1

Thinking: an overview

This chapter gives you some insights into thinking on a general level, and more specifically as it relates to the educational setting. I look at what exactly thinking is, examine the huge variety of ways in which you can use thinking in the classroom, and explore why thinking skills are so important. There's also plenty of information here about how to motivate your class in its thinking, and on how to pose questions in order to develop your children's thinking skills. This background knowledge should enable you to make better use of thinking within your own classroom, and within whatever area or areas of the curriculum you teach. The information contained in this first chapter will help you access and use the material that makes up the rest of the book.

What is thinking?

In scientific terms, thinking is a physical process. We are born with billions of cells called neurons, which have the capacity to help us think and learn. For our brains to work properly, these neurons have to connect with each other, so that they can pass electrical impulses from cell to cell. As we grow and experience the world in which we live, a process called myelination occurs. During this process the neurons in our brains are coated with myelin, and this helps with the transfer of these electrical impulses.

Connections in the brain are made in two ways: first, by inter-acting with our environment, and second by the normal matur-ing of the brain. The more opportunities for stimulation and active exploration a child has, the better these connections will be formed and maintained. Once the neurons are connected together, a network of pathways in the brain is formed. As these pathways are used repeatedly, the connections become a perma-nent part of our brains.

It has been shown that our brains have two sides – left and right – each of which controls a different type of thought. The left side of the brain is involved with the more academically based aspects of thinking, such as logic, reasoning, analysis and numbers. The right side of the brain deals with the more creative areas of thought. These include imagination, colour, rhythm, the ability to see the whole picture, and so on. It is generally accepted that most individuals tend to be more right- or left-brain dominant. This goes some way towards explaining why some of us are so much better at maths and other logically based subjects and others excel in the more creative areas of the curriculum, such as English and art.

That's the science over and done with! On a more philosophi-cal level, thinking is what differentiates humans from animals, giving us a sense of self (and of other selves). The fact that we can use conscious thought allows us to do so many of the things that make the human race unique. We can plan ahead, devise logical solutions to the problems that we encounter, develop complex belief systems, create wonderful stories, music and art, make interpretations of texts that we read, and so on.

As I mentioned in the Introduction, one of the problems that teachers face with thinking is that it is an invisible activity – one that takes place solely inside each individual's mind. Although it is possible to make the thinking process visible, for instance by using discussion tasks, it is fairly difficult to quantify exactly what is being achieved when our students do their thinking. You'll find lots of ideas in this book about ways in which you can make thinking a more visible aspect of your classroom practice. You'll also find some tips about how you can assess the thinking that your students undertake.

There can be a tendency to view thinking as a process that involves words, whether this is in our students' heads, through discussion tasks or written on the page. However, there is much more to thinking than this. For instance, athletes are now using the power of positive thinking to improve their performances. By visualizing a successful approach, whether in scoring a goal, clearing a high jump, or running a faster race, improvements have been made at the highest levels of athletic endeavour. Thinking is also about exploring some of the constructs that human beings have put upon their world. We might be looking at how and why numbers work, exploring how colour and shape can be used to create art, seeing how notes can be put together to create a harmonious piece of music, and so on.

An important part of the development of thinking is the ability to use metacognition. This complicated-sounding word simply describes the process by which we think about how we think. In this book you will notice how I spend quite some time talking about my own mental processes during the act of writing and organizing the material that I have included. My aim in doing this is to help you understand and use metacognition better in your own classroom.

Different experts and authorities divide thinking up into many different areas, categories and skills. I've listed just a few of the terms that you may come across when studying the area of thinking below. It is also my aim in this book to demystify all these terms: to show you exactly how you might approach the different types of thinking in your classroom, and to give you a variety of tasks that you can use in so doing.

✓ logic;
✓ reasoning;
✓ memory;
✓ evaluative thinking;
✓ creative thinking;
✓ critical thinking;
✓ philosophical thinking.

Why is thinking important?

Thinking is important both within the educational setting, and also in our students' wider lives outside school. Being able to think clearly, logically and also creatively is fundamental to a successful approach to life. Within the classroom thinking is important for a whole host of reasons. First and foremost, thinking allows our children to approach the work we set in a conscious way, rather than simply learning by rote. This has a number of benefits for both teacher and student:

- *A sense of ownership:* It is really important that our children feel that they have ownership of their own learning. It is incredibly motivating for students to discover a fresh topic for themselves, or to think up new and original ideas and inventions. Some of the big philosophical questions allow our children to feel a powerful sense of ownership – there is no real 'right' or 'wrong' when discussing philosophy, simply different views and opinions of what is 'true' and 'real'.
- *Applying what is learnt and thought:* Our aim should be for our students to learn through self-discovery and by thinking for themselves, rather than by being told. If we can achieve this, they will be far more likely to be able to apply their new-found knowledge or skills to other areas of their learning. This ability to apply what is learnt and thought will stand them in good stead throughout their lives, not just during their school days.
- *A sense of individuality:* Thought is a totally individual process – no two people think in the same way, or have the same thoughts and ideas. Consequently, developing our students' thinking skills allows us to give them a sense of themselves as individual learners and thinkers. For instance, in the arenas of creativity and invention an original and individual approach is highly prized and valued.
- *Fitting the work to the class:* Learning in a conscious way, and by discovery, helps the teacher work from where the class already is at any given point in time, rather than starting from scratch. Approaching topics via thinking skills allows us to find out

4

what our children already know, and add to this previous knowledge or ability level.

- *Fitting the work to the individual:* On a similar note, thinking skills give us a wonderful opportunity to differentiate the work for our children. One student might think only at the most basic level whereas another might take his or her thinking to a much higher and more complex standard. Bear in mind that this will not necessarily correlate with how academically able the students are – the ability to use your brain effectively is about so much more than IQ.

Thinking skills can have a very positive impact on our students' approaches to their learning, as I have explained above. They will also provide benefits on a much wider scale, helping our children in their lives both inside and outside school. The following points cover just some of the ways in which these benefits might be felt.

- *Conceptualizing:* Being able to think effectively, and to make connections between different thoughts or experiences, is essential in the development and understanding of concepts. For instance, when they first start school our children do not yet understand that the Earth is a large planet in an infinite universe. At this stage, their experience is mainly of the local area in which they live and there is little point in teaching them about the geography of other countries. This conceptual development is vital both inside and outside school. To give just one example, until children understand the concept of empathy (see below), they may not behave in an appropriate way towards others. When they have grasped this particular concept they will be able to start to behave in a way that our society finds acceptable.
- *Empathizing:* Thinking is a vital part of developing empathy with other people. This is a skill that develops over time and with practice. It is only once our children develop empathy, and learn to think about how their actions and behaviour affect others, that they can develop proper socialization. The first concept that we grasp, right at the earliest stage in our lives, is that other people have a 'self' apart from us. Only then do we

understand that other people can feel emotions such as sadness, happiness, anger or hurt. This understanding plays a crucial part in developing and maintaining good relationships, both within the classroom and also in the world outside school.

- *Developing morality:* Traditional religions do provide many of our children with a moral code for their lives. However, with the growth of a secular society there is a need to find a moral pathway through thinking about the 'big' questions, as well as through religious training. It is also important for those who are being brought up within a particular faith to be able to understand the moral tenets of their religion, and also to understand and perhaps question why these are accepted. Our children need to understand the whole range of religious thoughts and beliefs, and to see why some people believe in a different way of life from their own. If we can harness the power of thinking to help them do this we will hopefully play our part in creating a more tolerant and accepting society.

- *Dealing with the 'big' issues:* In addition to exploring religious beliefs, thinking also allows us to come to our own decisions about the 'big' questions of life. Early on, our children may simply take on the beliefs and ideas of their parents. However, by the time they reach secondary school, and probably long before, they will be asking themselves those age-old questions such as *'Is there a God?'* and *'What happens when I die?'* Such questions can actually be a source of worry and even fear for our students, particularly those who have been encouraged to believe that the answers are set in stone. As teachers, we can provide them with a safe environment for developing their own ideas and questioning what others tell them, in order to find out what they really believe.

- *Common sense:* Thinking skills allow us to develop a common-sense and practical approach to life. In school, or later on when they move out into the real world, our children will constantly face problems that need solving. Finding practical and common-sense solutions to the issues we encounter is a vital part of learning how to deal with life. In fact, this common-sense approach plays a big part in my whole attitude towards teaching, especially when it comes to dealing with behaviour.

The ideas that I put forward in books such as *Getting the Buggers to Behave* are based on common-sense approaches that actually work in the classroom. Although theory has its place, it is common sense that I believe really makes the biggest impact in the running of our daily lives.

- *Concentration and focus:* One of the most important factors in good-quality thinking is the ability to concentrate and focus to a high standard. I've devoted the whole of the next chapter to this area, and this reflects the importance I place on it. Clearly, if our students can develop good concentration and focus, this will have a huge impact on their learning throughout the whole of their educational experience. It will also pay dividends in terms of their chances of success after they leave school.

Thinking in the classroom

It is not necessarily the most intelligent children who are the best at thinking. Some children are very good at taking a common-sense and logical approach to the issues and problems they face, even though they might not necessarily be the brightest students in an academic sense. Other children are extremely talented at working within a group, particularly on the discussion tasks that play such a vital role in developing thinking skills. When you are approaching thinking in your own classroom, do bear in mind that different students will be good at different types of thinking. Some will be good at working out mathematical puzzles, others will be brilliant at solving mysteries, some will be able to discuss philosophical questions in depth and with sensitivity, others will be bundles of creative and imaginative energy.

Although our children will be starting from different levels of ability, it is, of course, possible to develop the thinking skills of every student. For instance, in a whole class discussion the quieter individuals may not actually make many verbal contributions, but they will hopefully be taking on board the ideas and suggestions that are made by their classmates. We as teachers can assist every child in learning how to think better. In order to do this, we need to make the processes of thinking as explicit as possible, mapping out the different structures and approaches for the class in clear detail (for example, showing them how memory systems work, and so on).

You will find lots of ideas below about how thinking can be used and developed in the classroom. These points deal mainly with the organizational issues connected to teaching thinking skills, looking at the classroom management factors involved. Further on, you will find plenty of advice about helping your children to structure their thinking, and how to develop thought in all its myriad forms.

How can I develop my students' thinking skills?

Thinking skills can be taught both as a discrete curriculum area but also (and mainly) as an integral part of all the subjects of the curriculum. Of course, we would hope that thinking is taking place throughout every single lesson that we teach, although some lessons will obviously encourage more independent thought or detailed thinking than others. When you are aiming to develop your students' thinking skills, the following tips and points should be of assistance.

- *The importance of discussion:* Discussion really does play an absolutely vital part in the development of thinking. It allows our students to practise so many vital skills: to test their ideas out loud; to gain and learn through feedback from their peers; to develop a thought by adding a number of different people's ideas together; to learn how to structure their ideas in a coherent way. You find ideas throughout this book for encouraging high-quality discussions.
- *Get them in the mood:* Before decent-quality thought can take place, it is essential that we get our children in the right mood to think. This might be as simple as gaining their attention for an explanation of the task, or encouraging them to concentrate properly when they do a thinking exercise. It might also involve the teacher thinking carefully about the atmosphere in the room – for instance, ensuring that there is quiet so that they

can work well. It could even mean creating a 'special' atmosphere for an activity, such as the use of darkness and torches for thinking about and working with ghost stories and the supernatural. You can find lots of ideas about getting your class in the right mood for work in Chapter 2, which looks at the links between good concentration and behaviour and high-quality thought.

- *Give them free rein:* Some of the most original and interesting thoughts come about when we are given the freedom to think 'outside the box'. What this means is when we allow ourselves and our students to think in unconventional ways – for instance, approaching a commonplace problem from an unusual angle. In order to do this, you need to be willing to give your children free rein when it comes to their thinking. Naturally, some of the tasks you set will be fairly tightly structured. However, for the majority of thinking tasks it is best for the teacher to give the children the freedom for their thoughts to wander, at least a little.
- *No right or wrong:* Unlike some areas of teaching, much thinking is not about yes or no answers. Although there will obviously be some puzzles or sums to which a correct answer can be found, many activities that you set, or questions that you pose, will allow for a huge range of possible approaches and solutions. You will probably need to explain this to your children. The current emphasis on quantifying and testing skills and knowledge means that they could already be set in the belief that you want specific answers to the questions you ask. Making it clear that there is no right or wrong answer will free them up to be as creative as possible in their approaches to thinking and learning.

How can I motivate my children to think?

Having looked at what thinking is, and why it is so important, we also need to take into account the importance of actually motivating our children to think. It is no good simply sitting them down and saying *'I want you to think about this.'* For a start, many of them will have no idea about how to structure their thoughts (see

Chapter 3 for some useful hints about how to develop this area). Those children who find it hard to focus and behave well do need to be highly motivated if they are going to stay on task and if the thinking that takes place is going to be of value. We need to actually encourage them to see thinking as an interesting and rewarding activity in its own right. Here are some ideas about how you can do this.

- *Make thinking rewarding:* Rewards come in many shapes and sizes. Although we might tend to think first of material rewards, such as merit marks and stickers, children are in fact often best rewarded simply by a teacher who lavishes praise on them. When one of your students comes up with an original or interesting thought, make a song and dance about it. The really good thing about thinking is that children can be as 'good' (or better) at it than adults. You might say something like: *'That's a really great idea – I would never have thought of looking at the problem in that way.'*
- *Make thinking a challenge:* When you are trying to develop your children's motivation one of the most useful approaches is to set them challenges. This brings out the natural competitiveness of our students and is as useful in encouraging good thinking as it is in developing good behaviour. Here are some tips on how to make thinking a challenge for your children:
  - o *Find the biggest number:* In my experience, children love challenges that ask them to come up with more 'x' than each other. This might mean setting them a problem and then challenging them to see who can come up with the greatest number of different solutions. For instance, in a maths lesson, you could ask the class to come up with the most different sums that can make the number 100, using only the minus and plus signs.
  - o *Find the most original . . .:* Similarly, you could challenge your students to see who can be the most original and imaginative child in the class. An example could be seeing who can think of the most original use for an empty plastic bottle.
  - o *Set a time challenge:* Children also respond really well to being challenged to complete an activity within a set period of

time. Often, the shorter the time period, the better the students' motivation and focus will be. Your time challenge might be to see who can be the quickest to complete a task, but you could also give the class a set period within which everyone has to finish an exercise. An excellent idea for making time challenges more concrete is to use a short piece of music (such as the theme from *Mission Impossible*) to give a time frame for finishing the work.

- *Make the thinking achievable:* Of course, there is no point at all in setting our children thinking tasks that are completely out of reach, as this will only end up demotivating them. On the other hand, I have always found my students best motivated by activities that I might have imagined would be too hard for them. The key for the teacher is to find a balance. You need to make the tasks difficult enough to provide a challenge, but not so complex or hard to complete that they put off the less able thinker right from the word go. It is actually worth making it clear to your students how far you are challenging them, as this will demonstrate your belief in their abilities. I might say something to my class like, *'This is a really hard task, but I know how clever and keen you all are, so I'm sure you'll be able to do it.'*

- *Show them how the techniques work:* When you set a difficult task, this gives you the perfect opportunity to introduce your children to ways of enhancing their ability to think. Some of the structures and approaches that can be used are surprisingly simple but will make a huge difference to the end result. Showing your students just how these techniques can be used will play a huge part in helping motivate them in their thinking. For instance, if you ask them to memorize a number of objects, they might find the task very hard at first. However, by teaching them a simple memory system such as that described in Chapter 5, you will help them find the key to better quality thought.

- *Use the power of mystery:* Children (and indeed adults) love mysteries. As teachers we can use this enjoyment to better motivate our students. Starting a lesson by setting up a mystery, for instance using the crime scene exercise described in Chapter 6, will immediately hook your children into the work. And once they are hooked, their motivation to complete the work will be high. You will find a full explanation of using mystery to develop thinking skills in Chapter 6.

- *Integrate thinking into all your lessons:* Our aim should be for our children to come to see thinking as an integral part of every lesson we teach. Rather than the old-fashioned approach of learning by rote, the thinking class explores how ideas, techniques, experiments, and so on actually work. To give an example, in a 'rote' chemistry lesson you might present the students with a worksheet describing how two chemicals should be mixed together, what will happen when they are mixed, and why this is so. The class then goes about following the worksheet to complete the experiment. However, in a 'thinking' chemistry lesson, the class might instead be asked to come up with a hypothesis about what it thinks will happen when two chemicals are mixed together. The children could spend some time working out their own theories, then go on to experiment using different approaches and techniques.

- *Have 'thinking time':* Just as primary school teachers are asked to dedicate an hour to literacy, so we might choose to devote a specific amount of time to thinking, and set aside this thinking time within each lesson. By doing this, you will demonstrate to your students just how valuable you believe thinking to be. You will also put yourself into a position whereby you allocate and use a decent quantity of time on developing thinking skills.

- *Allow time for free thought:* With all the pressures to work through the statutory curriculum, it is tempting to try and fit thinking into a strict time frame. Unfortunately for the hard-pressed teacher, this is not quite how thinking works. Some of the best thinking will be done when your children are allowed the time to let their minds roam free for a while, when the task set is vague, allowing as much room as possible for unusual and original thought. Giving your children the time to think deeply and freely will, of course, have benefits for the rest of their learning. It will also help to motivate them by allowing them the freedom to extend and expand their minds. The teacher needs to be brave, and to believe that the benefits outweigh the potential cost of spending a lot of time on such an apparently nebulous activity.

- *Allow them to think weird thoughts:* The effective thinker is not afraid to think weird or unusual things, to see where these thoughts might lead. As we saw in the previous section, thinking is not necessarily about right and wrong answers. Some of the 'best' thoughts happen when we think 'outside the box', when we are not scared to think unusual things, or to take new and original approaches. Again, this will help engage your children with the thinking work that you do.

- *Inspire them!* The best teachers are not only excellent classroom managers, but are also a source of inspiration for their children. We can inspire our students by showing them our passion for the whole process of learning. We can also inspire them by using original and exciting approaches to our lesson planning when it comes to choosing and structuring thinking tasks. For instance, you might bring in an unusual object to inspire your children's thoughts. This could be as bizarre as the teacher bringing in a bicycle wheel and then posing the question *'Could wheels be any other shape but round, and what would happen if they were?'* (See the point below on using objects to get some more ideas about this approach.) By inspiring and engaging our classes in this way, we will certainly encourage them to see thinking as fun and exciting.

- *Be a role model:* Believe it or not, many children do look up to their teachers, and will often emulate the role model that you provide for them. This being the case, it is important that you articulate your own thought processes for the class and that you show how motivated you are by the whole area of thinking. You can do this by using sentences with the words 'think', 'thought', and so on and by making it clear that you find the work interesting. Tell the class what you are thinking about when you teach, and also make clear the thoughts that lead you to set particular activities. Involve your children in the thinking process, for instance, by allowing them to have some impact on the way that your lessons progress. Here are just some of the phrases that you might use to do this:

- o *'I was thinking about all the different and exciting ways that we could approach this topic. I came up with these three ideas. Which do you think is best?'*
- o *'In my opinion you've all done some really good work today, I'm so pleased with what you've achieved. What do you think was most successful about your thinking and learning in this lesson?'*
- o *'What do you think an appropriate homework would be for this lesson? The person who makes the best suggestion gets to be teacher and set the class its homework.'*
- o *'Where do you think we might go next with this topic to keep it interesting for us? What are your thoughts about a suitable follow-up lesson?'*
- *Use objects:* It really is very motivating for our students to see 'things' in the classroom that are not normally there. These objects become props that bring the learning to life for the children, giving them an added motivation and a concrete basis for their thinking. To give just one example, the teacher might open a lesson by bringing in a coconut and asking the children to use it as a basis for some thinking. The possible curriculum areas that this could inspire vary widely – from geography to English, from art to music. Here are just a few thoughts on the type of questions that your coconut might elicit.
  - o *'What sort of country do you think this fruit comes from?'*
  - o *'How do you think this grows – is it on a tree, or a plant, or under the ground?'*
  - o *'What sort of weather conditions do you think it needs to grow?'*
  - o *'Why do you think it has a thick brown husk?'*
  - o *'Why do you think it grows in this particular shape?'*
  - o *'How could we open the coconut? Think of ten different ways.'*
  - o *'How would we open it if we didn't have any man-made tools?'*
  - o *'Which senses can we use in response to the coconut?'*
  - o *'How could we use it to make a musical instrument?'*
  - o *'How can we use it to make an eating vessel?'*
  - o *'What else could we make with this coconut?'*

The importance of questioning

Questions play a vital role in the development of thinking. By posing questions to the students, and asking them to come up with answers, they develop a whole array of different thinking skills. They might learn how to solve problems, how to explore ethical and moral issues, how to develop their creativity, and so on. It is important therefore for us to think carefully about:

- the type of questions we ask;
- the way that we pose these questions;
- the way that our children ask questions of each other;
- how we encourage our students to work out their answers;
- how we can help our children structure their answers.

Here are some sample 'starter' questions that you might use in the classroom to encourage your students to develop better and wider thinking skills.

- *'What would happen if . . .?'*
- *'How could we do this differently . . .?'*
- *'How could we do this better . . .?'*
- *'What's going on here . . .?'*
- *'What is this person trying to tell us . . .?'*
- *'How well does this work . . .?'*
- *'How can I persuade someone to . . .?'*
- *'What do I already know about this topic . . .?'*
- *'How should I structure my answer . . .?'*

Questioning can be divided into two main 'types' – the open and the closed question. An explanation of each type is given below. Some questions will fall between the two types. For instance, the question *'Is there a God?'* could be answered as a closed question with a simple 'yes' or 'no'. However, it would normally be treated as an open question, which would elicit a more detailed and thoughtful response. (A third type of question, the rhetorical question, is a great favourite with teachers – *'Do you really want to do that?'* – not actually requiring or expecting an answer!)

Open questions

An open question is one that does not have a set or correct answer, but rather a whole range of possible replies. These questions are excellent for developing our students' thinking skills as they allow for detailed exploration of an issue, problem or other point that you might pose. Open questions encourage the children to look at a subject from all sides and to take a variety of approaches in finding an answer. In fact, you should find that you end up with as many, or more, different answers or solutions as there are children in the class. There are a number of points to consider when using open questioning in your teaching.

- These questions help to encourage the searching, comprehensive, imaginative, intuitive and individual side of our personalities.
- At their best, they encourage the children to respond with creativity and by using complex, higher-order thought processes.
- Asking an open question will tend to lead to more lengthy discussions than will a closed question.
- Ideas that come about as a result of the initial question could well lead to other different questions and jumps in the children's chain of thought.
- When leading a session of open questioning, the teacher can use further questions to move the discussion along.

Here are some tips on using open questions in your classroom:

- *Take your time:* When posing an open question, do ensure that there is sufficient time and opportunity for discussion work (or written answers) to take place. It is a real shame to ask an open question that encourages really interesting responses only to have to shut down the children's thought processes just as they get going because the bell has rung for break. On the other hand, sometimes having a short period of really focused discussion will be just what you want. See 'Set the limits' below for more thoughts on this.
- *Use a process of development:* Try to respond to your children's initial answers by encouraging them to develop their thinking

16

further. This development might move with one single thought to its conclusion, or it could step sideways, as lateral thought. You will probably need to pose additional questions to elicit this development, such as *'Why do you think that?'* and *'How can we take that idea further?'* Your aim should be to develop a purposeful dialogue, and to encourage clarity of thought from the class. This might involve you leading the thinking in appropriate directions, or asking the children to support their thoughts with suitable evidence, and to find the logical conclusions to their train of thinking. See the sample discussion below to get some more ideas about how you can fully develop your children's thinking processes.

- *Make the process explicit:* As you go through the question with your students, you can play an important role in helping to make their thinking processes explicit. This metacognition plays a vital part in the development of high quality learning through thinking activities. To give an example, making the process explicit might involve the teacher explaining how the discussion is progressing, for instance by pointing out lateral jumps in the thought patterns which are taking place.

- *Involve the children:* Open questions do not always have to be posed by the teacher. In fact, involving your students in the setting as well as the answering of questions is an excellent way to get them thinking. You might set a general topic, for instance 'The way we treat our environment', and then ask the children to come up with a number of questions that they would like to discuss.

- *Be positive and supportive:* Children can be very sensitive about their ideas, and may well feel nervous about making what they see as unusual or off-the-wall contributions. Your aim is to encourage them in taking the thinking in whatever directions occur to them, so you will need to be as positive and supportive as possible. Try to avoid making negative comments, even when a child's thoughts don't seem to make any sense. Instead, use words such as *'interesting'*, *'original'* and *'thought-provoking'* in response. In any event, it is often the case that the most illogical or weird-sounding thoughts are actually very useful in taking the thinking to a higher level.

- *Watch your vocabulary:* The way in which we phrase our questions has a fundamental impact on the way that our children will answer and also on how well they will develop thinking within the class. As you pose questions to your children take a moment to listen to the way in which you set them. Consider too whether you have a specific response in mind, and are simply asking the question in order to elicit this particular answer.
- *Get them all talking:* Open questions might be used within a whole class session, but it's also a great (if noisy) idea to get all the children discussing a single question at once. You might specify some individual thinking time before the chatting begins, or you could just let the class loose straight away.
- *Set the limits:* Sometimes, it can help to set very tight limits when the children are discussing their answers to an open question. These limits really help to focus the discussion, and they also show the class how we can give a clear structure to our thinking. You might set a single constraint, such as a short period of time in which to formulate an answer. Alternatively, you might combine a couple of the suggestions below, for instance giving the class two minutes in which to come up with the three best ideas. Here are some ideas for setting limits:
  o *Time limits* – give the children two minutes to talk about the topic, then move on. (They don't necessarily have to come up with a fully formulated answer.)
  o *Idea limits* – ask the groups to narrow down their discussion, and end up with the three best ideas that were found.
  o *Word limits* – tell the children that they each have exactly 20 words in which to explain their answer to your question (not a word more or less!).
  o *Sentence limits* – ask the students to say one sentence each on the question, moving around in a circle so that everyone has a chance to contribute.
- *Obtain some feedback:* After a session in which all your students have been talking about their ideas, it's very useful to get some feedback from them. You might ask each group to make a few quick comments, going round the class to see what issues have been raised. Alternatively, you could set a task that involves preparing a longer verbal presentation. You might also ask for

written feedback that can be photocopied and shared with the class. There are a number of reasons why it's such a good idea to get feedback after a questioning session.

o It allows the class to share the different ideas which came up during the discussion.

o It lets the children (and the teacher) see all the different directions in which a single open question might lead them.

o It encourages the groups (or individuals) to crystallize their thinking and to come up with some specific points which they view as the most important.

o It helps the students learn how to structure their thoughts so that they can be best communicated to others.

Some examples of open questions include:

- *'What is good?'*
- *'How can we approach this task/problem/experiment differently?'*
- *'Should children be forced to come to school?'*
- *'What can we make out of this empty plastic bottle?'*

Below is a sample from a discussion on the question *'What is good?'* You'll see the teacher helping the children to develop and clarify their ideas, to keep the thoughts on track, and also to move laterally from the starting point. It is interesting to note how much of the time the teacher is posing further questions in response to what the students say. The comments given in square brackets explain the different ways in which the teacher helps facilitate the discussion.

Teacher:	What is good?
Student 1:	Is it the opposite of bad?
Teacher:	That certainly can be true. Does anybody else have any other thoughts on what we mean by 'good'?
Student 2:	It's when somebody does the right thing.
Teacher:	That's an interesting point. But what do you mean by the right thing?

[The teacher encourages the student to clarify his suggestion and develop the point further.]

Student 2:	Like when you're nice to people, or when you help somebody who's being bullied.
Student 3:	Or you can be good if somebody asks you to steal with them, and you say no.
Student 4:	And if you give money to charity, that's being good.
Teacher:	Those are all excellent ideas. So, people can be good. Can the word 'good' mean anything else? Can it relate to anything other than people?

[The teacher encourages the class to move laterally from this opening.]

Student 2:	It can be when you do good work, and the teacher gives you a merit mark.
Teacher:	And what do we mean by 'good work'? What sort of things would I give you a merit mark for?

[Again, the teacher encourages the children to support and develop the statements that they make.]

Student 3:	It has to be correct, to give the right answers.
Student 1:	And it has to be neat and look nice.
Teacher:	But can a piece of work be 'good' without being neat? What if the ideas that you had included were really imaginative?
Student 1:	That would still be good but not as good as it could be.
Student 4:	I got a merit mark for my homework, and you wrote 'This is excellent work' on it.
Teacher:	So there are other words that mean the same as 'good', aren't there? Can anyone give me some more examples?

[The teacher gets the class thinking about the word itself to see where this might lead them.]

Student 5:	Lovely, excellent.
Student 2:	Brilliant, superb.
Student 3:	Miss, good sounds a bit like God, doesn't it?
Teacher:	That's a brilliant thought, well done, I really like that idea. Let's think about that for a while – how

do you think the word 'good' relates to the word 'God'?

[The teacher helps the students to move laterally with this thought to see where it might go.]

Student 3:   God is good, isn't he miss?

Student 1:   And he makes people be good, otherwise he sends them to Hell.

Student 4:   Or he shoots them with a lightning bolt. That's why people are good, because they're scared.

Teacher: So people are good to each other because they're worried about what God might do to them if they're not? Is that always the case? Does everyone think that's correct?

Student 5:   My mum says there's no such thing as God, miss.

Teacher: Yes, that's what some people believe. Let's think about that for a while. Can people be good if they don't believe in God?

Student 5:   My mum's good.

Teacher: I'm sure she is. So, why would people be good if they're not scared about getting on the wrong side of God?

[The discussion has now moved to a philosophical and moral debate about the nature of good and bad as it concerns humanity!]

Closed questions

Research has shown that teachers often rely rather heavily on closed questions, and tend to use more of them than open questions. Thinking about my own style in the classroom, I know that I am guilty of this! The temptation is to ask the students questions to which we expect a specific response and to which we already know the required answer. Obviously, there will be times when we want or need to ask closed questions, for instance in a test where we wish to check our children's understanding of a factual topic area. However, it is important to balance these closed questions with sessions where we use a more open approach to our questioning, particularly if we wish to develop higher-order thinking skills.

21

With closed questions, any thinking that does take place will come about as the children try to find the correct answer to the query you have set. If the students have retained the facts that they need, or if they already understand how to do a calculation that you've asked them to do, then the thinking that occurs is the process of remembering the information and working out the answer.

When using closed questions it is important to consider the issue of differentiation. The problem is that some of your more academic students will know the answer to your closed question pretty much instantaneously. Their hands shoot up and it is very tempting to ask these keen children to give the answer. This means that those students who are a bit slower on the uptake can sit back and not raise their hands, allowing the bright sparks to do all the work. Of course, if the questions are written down then differentiation will take place through the individual working out the answers in his or her own time. On the whole, though, a classroom where open questions are used more frequently than closed ones will tend to encourage and develop a wider range of thinking skills.

Here are some examples of closed questions to show you what I mean.

- *'How many red blocks are there in the box?'*
- *'What was the name of the first king of England?'*
- *'What is 2 + 2?'*
- *'Who is the author of the Harry Potter books?'*

As you can see, these questions require either pre-existing knowledge, or the ability to use certain skills or techniques, such as being able to add up. In summary, the key for the teacher is to try to balance the two types of questioning and to be aware of when he or she is focusing too heavily on either open or closed questions.

2

Thinking: concentration, behaviour and learning

This chapter deals with the fundamentals of being able to think – the approaches and behaviour that must be in place before we can expect high quality thinking to take place. Learning how to concentrate is absolutely vital for developing thinking skills, and this is an area in which many of our students struggle. Good behaviour, and a focus on the work at hand, are also essential factors in getting our children to think, and to think properly. You'll find lots of thoughts, ideas and strategies in this chapter to help you understand the need and requirements for good levels of concentration, and also to create the appropriate climate in your classroom so that thinking can take place.

What is concentration?

When I run training courses for teachers, one of the most common complaints I hear is that some of their children simply cannot concentrate for any decent length of time. This lack of concentration tends to manifest itself through off-task behaviour, such as being unable to listen to the teacher's instructions in silence, chatting when they should be working, or getting up and wandering around the classroom. It might also be apparent in an inability to finish the work, or in a failure to complete activities to the required standard. Often, we will see that a child has huge potential and is incredibly bright but, because of a lack of concentration, he or she simply does not fulfil this potential. Poor concentration can be very annoying for the teacher (and for the other students), not least because it interferes with the ability of the whole class to focus on the work they should be doing. Good concentration is absolutely essential for good quality learning, and nowhere is this more so than when we are asking our children to think.

What, then, do we actually mean by 'concentration'? At the simplest level, concentration is the ability to focus on one thing, to the exclusion of all distractions. This single-minded focus is absolutely vital when it comes to getting our students to develop their thinking skills. Unfortunately for us, schools are full of distractions – from the temptation for children to send texts on their mobiles or chat with their classmates, to the sound of a noisy class next door. Our children need to learn how to block out all the other, extraneous thoughts that are filling their minds. These thoughts might include distractions within the class and also worries from the wider world outside the school gates.

The ancient art of meditation provides a very useful method of training ourselves to focus on one thing for a lengthy period of time. Although meditation is traditionally associated with religious training, particularly in the Eastern faiths, it is also a skill that can be used to great effect in the classroom. As you'll see below in 'Exercises for concentration', teaching your students how to meditate can lead to better concentration and it can also be good fun for both the teacher and the children.

Why do some children find it hard to concentrate?

There is no doubt that some of our students do find it incredibly difficult to concentrate in the classroom. This issue might manifest itself when they first start at school: for example, the nursery or reception age child who finds it impossible to sit still on the carpet when the teacher is reading a story. It may also be a problem that reoccurs throughout their school careers and if it is not solved it can have a hugely detrimental impact on their educational success. When invigilating GCSE exams I have witnessed the sad sight of a student who knows how important these tests are but who simply finds it impossible to focus attention on the vital task at hand. There are a whole host of reasons why our students do find it so difficult to concentrate. These include:

- *A lack of early training:* The young child needs to learn how to concentrate, gradually increasing the length and intensity of his or her focus. Some of the children we teach, particularly those from a background of poor parenting skills, may never have learned to concentrate on one thing for any length of time. It could be that the parents have never introduced the idea of concentrated playing or working with a single object or on a specific activity. It might be that the child has been over-stimulated, given a number of toys at any one time, without the requirement to develop focused play. This perhaps particularly applies to those children who have been encouraged to sit in front of the television or computer games for long periods of time, and who have consequently become accustomed to high-level stimulation without the need for concentrated thought.

- *Special needs:* For those students with special needs, particularly behavioural problems such as attention deficit hyperactivity disorder (ADHD), concentration is a real area of weakness in their development. This is especially so for the hyperactive child who is unable to sit still for any length of time, and who finds it very difficult to concentrate. When considering how to develop thinking skills in your classroom, do take into account the particular needs of those children who have learning difficulties. In these circumstances, you will need to adapt the approaches you use, for instance, by introducing gradually increasing periods of concentrated work.

- *Lack of engagement with the learning:* If we ask our children to complete tasks that they find boring and mundane, without any interest in or reward for doing so, then it is hardly surprising if they find it hard to concentrate. For some of our students, this lack of engagement manifests itself in a total disaffection with education as a whole. For others, the problem is only with specific subjects, teachers or topics. If we wish to develop better concentration in our classrooms, and consequently to encourage strong thinking skills, then it is essential that we engage our students with the learning. You'll find lots of ideas for engaging classroom tasks in this book, to help you encourage the disaffected students that you teach.

- *Problems inside the classroom:* In some cases, the classroom is simply not a place which is conducive to quality thinking. It could be that your class has particularly poor behaviour, or that you teach a very noisy bunch of youngsters. If this is the case, it will be very hard for the students not to become distracted when they are meant to be deep in thought. Other problems within the classroom setting might include a cluttered and untidy environment, excessive heat, or simply a lack of space to work. Again, you will need to take these factors into account when teaching your students how to think.

- *Problems outside the classroom:* If a child is experiencing difficulties in the home environment then this will inevitably have an effect on his or her levels of concentration in the classroom. It's the classic saying – 'my mind was elsewhere'. When we have something serious to worry about, it becomes very hard to keep our minds focused on school work, which may seem rather trivial in comparison. Similarly, issues within the school setting but outside the classroom may also have an impact on levels of concentration in your lessons. For instance, if a child has just broken up with a circle of close friends, or is being bullied, then it is possible that he or she might demonstrate poor concentration when it comes to work in the classroom.

Exercises for concentration

When you're aiming to develop your students' concentration skills there is a whole range of activities that you can use in your quest. The exercises described in this section will help you to develop better concentration skills within your class or classes. Before you put the exercises into use, it is worth taking some time to consider how you should approach them. Here are some tips that will help you use them in the most effective way.

- *A gradual build up:* When you first introduce these activities, do bear in mind that, to start off with, the children will find it hard to focus properly for a good length of time. Don't expect instant results, especially from a class that does not normally demonstrate good concentration skills. Build the exercises up gradually: for instance, start by setting the 'statues' activity (see below) for only a minute, before moving on to two minutes, then three, and so on. Eventually you will find your children are able to concentrate for long periods of time.

- *Explain your expectations:* One of the best ways to encourage our children to do well at the tasks we give them is to set our expectations at a very high level. Share your high expectations with your class – for instance, tell them that you know that they will be able to do the exercise extremely well. If the students don't live up to your expectations, don't get angry with them; instead express surprise at how they have failed to achieve the results of which you know they are capable.

- *Make it a challenge:* In order to encourage your students to do their best in these exercises, present the activities as a challenge or even as a test. Explain to your children that you know they will be able to do these activities very well (see 'Explain your expectations' above), and this is why you are able to set them such a difficult challenge to complete. A useful tip for secondary teachers is to use the example of another class that you teach to set the children a benchmark to aim for. For instance, you could tell a Year 7 class that your Year 9 class can do the statues exercise for two whole minutes (children do love to 'beat' their older counterparts!). By presenting them with a challenge you will encourage their sense of competition and help them strive to achieve even better results.

- *Reward them:* Introduce the idea that good concentration will be rewarded, both by you as a teacher, and also in the educational success which is the reward for high levels of focus. You might offer a whole class reward for successful completion of two minutes as statues: for instance, the chance to take a two-minute 'time out' for a social chat. Alternatively you could offer individual rewards for those who complete the exercises the best, perhaps letting these students leave the lesson first

27

when the bell goes. One very useful individual reward is the chance for the children to 'be teacher' and run the next statues exercise themselves. Another good reward (and one that takes little effort or organization) is simply giving lavish praise to the class or individual.

Here are some examples of exercises that you can use to develop your students' concentration. I have used these activities with children of all ages – from reception class to sixth form, and even with teachers at the training sessions I run. Invariably, people love the chance to try out something a little different or unusual. Many of these exercises, in addition to teaching better concentration, will also help you develop other skills, such as listening and co-operation.

Meditation

Research has established that meditation has very beneficial effects on human beings. These effects include the obvious physical benefits such as relaxation and deep breathing. They also include intellectual bonuses, for instance, developing better concentration and the ability to dream up new ideas. The most difficult aspect of the art of meditation is the fact that it requires the total absence of thought, and this is in fact much harder than it sounds. In order to meditate we must put aside all those thoughts, images and words that tend to clutter up our heads. The mind should become a blank slate, taking the body into a deep mode of relaxation. There are various ways of introducing the skill of meditation at a basic level with your class. Rather than simply asking them to 'clear their minds', it is a good idea to start off by giving them something specific on which to focus. You should be able to adapt the ideas below according to the needs and abilities of your own children.

- *Focusing on an image:* When you ask your class to meditate, give them a specific image on which to concentrate their minds. For instance, they might imagine a clear blue sky in their heads, to help them keep a mental 'blank slate'. Ask the children to visualize any thoughts that do appear as clouds, which they can gently push away to help them maintain their clear blue sky.

- *Focusing on an object:* Another approach is to give your children an object to focus on. For example, you might hand out shells for the children to stare at. They can then 'lose' themselves by looking very deeply at the shells, studying the texture and colours very closely, or creating an image in their minds of where the shell was found. Alternatively, you might decide to use a picture as your object and ask the children to study it in depth, or to concentrate by staring at one tiny corner.

- *Using a chant:* Some people like to meditate by using a chant or a 'mantra'. Although traditionally associated with religious meditations, there is in fact no need for this chant to have any particular metaphysical significance. You might ask the children to choose words of their own, or you could ask the whole class to use the same word (for instance 'clear', 'soft' or 'calm'). The children can then chant the word over and over to help them clear their minds. If you feel a bit silly asking your students to chant a word out loud, they can instead simply say the word over and over in their heads.

- *Using music:* Music can provide us with a powerful focus for a meditation. Play a soft and calming piece of music to your class, preferably one without words. Ask the children to focus on the melody, or on the emotions it stirs, keeping any words or other thoughts out of their minds. The aim is for them to simply lose themselves in the music. You might ask them to imagine themselves as birds, swooping down and flying upwards again as the notes move up and down the scale.

Statues

This is one of my all-time favourite exercises. It has a huge range of benefits for the hard-pressed teacher. Not only does it develop the children's concentration but it gives you an opportunity for a relaxing few minutes of silence and stillness. I also find that the students really enjoy the chance to 'do nothing', and that they find it very relaxing too. The statues exercise provides an excellent way to finish off a lesson or to end up the school day – it is very calming and provides a lovely peaceful atmosphere in the classroom. You can take advantage of this silence to give any instructions, to set homework, or simply to praise your children for the good work they have done.

When I use the statues exercise described below to finish off a lesson, I like to end it by asking the children to place their chairs under the tables in slow motion. This helps maintain the calm feeling in the room right up to the end of the class. You can allow those who have done the activity best to do this first, and leave as soon as the bell goes as a reward for their high quality concentration. After a few tries at statues, you will soon find the class able to sustain their stillness for an impressively long time.

This is how the exercise works. Tell the children to make themselves comfortable (if you have a suitable space, it's an excellent idea for them to lie on a carpet). Then set them a challenge – they are going to freeze as still as statues for a specific length of time. At first, aim for only one or two minutes. They are allowed to breathe (obviously) but they should aim not to blink or to move any part of their bodies. Some of your children will find this surprisingly difficult. In fact, I'm always amazed by the link between those students who find this hardest, and those whose concentration skills are the weakest. As they hold their poses, keep giving them encouragement, noting how much time has passed and how much is still left to go. If you see a child moving slightly, try to give a non-verbal signal that you have noticed, rather than commenting in front of the whole class. Try also to develop the sense that the class is working as a unit to achieve the target you have set, as this will encourage those who find it most difficult to do better.

Focus exercises

The exercises described below are ones that I have used in drama lessons (and also in fact when doing supply cover in other subject areas). If you are working in a less artistic area of the curriculum, these exercises could be used as introduction to the lesson, or alternatively as a way of giving the class a break between different parts of the session. In the primary classroom, you might choose to start the day off with some focus exercises, perhaps repeating them after a break, when you need to get the children's minds back on their learning. Below are just a few examples of fun focus exercises. You'll also find a longer and more intensive focus exercise called 'Into the forest' in Chapter 7.

- *Hypnosis:* This exercise requires the students to maintain a focus on one thing for a certain period of time. (As we've established, this is one of the most essential skills required for concentration, and consequently an excellent preparation for deep thought.) The teacher should demonstrate the exercise first, by asking a student to come to the front of the class to be 'hypnotized'. I like to introduce this exercise by telling the class that I have magic powers, as this always gets their attention. Explain to the students that, when you click your fingers, they will be 'under your power'. Hold your palm up so that it is level with the child's face, and fairly close (about 20 cm away). The student must then follow you wherever you go, keeping his or her face at exactly the same distance from your hand. Move your hand around slowly, up and down, side to side, down to the floor, and so on. It always works well if, after demonstrating the exercise, you then let the volunteer hypnotize you in return. (The children love to see their teacher under a student's control!) This exercise can be done by the whole class simultaneously, working in pairs. If you're worried about keeping control with all the children being hypnotized at once, or if lack of space is an issue in your room, then ask half the class to do the exercise at one time. The rest of the class can watch to see who is doing the exercise best. Keep reminding your students that they are not trying to catch each other out and that the best way of doing the exercise is slowly and carefully, working with rather than against their partners.
- *Countdown:* This exercise helps your students calm themselves, and is very useful for gaining a class's focus at the start of a lesson and pulling them together, ready to work. Ask the children to shut their eyes, and then count backwards slowly from 50 to zero. When they reach zero, they should open their eyes, ready to begin.
- *Mental spelling:* This exercise is similar to the one described above and it also helps develop concentration and focus. Tell

your students to shut their eyes, and then spell a word or words backwards in their heads. For instance, you could start by asking them to spell their full names. Depending on their age, you could move on to more difficult words, perhaps connected to your subject area (for instance, in English 'onomatopoeia', in science 'invertebrate').

- *Listening:* Listening skills are very closely connected to thinking skills, because they play such an essential part in any discussions. Developing your children's ability to listen is also very useful for setting a calm and thoughtful atmosphere in the classroom. First of all, ask your children to simply close their eyes and listen to see what they can hear. Initially they could focus on sounds within the classroom, gradually moving out to sounds in the corridors, and then around the school. Set a time limit, perhaps two minutes, and afterwards talk with your students to find out what they heard. You might set a challenge to see who can hear the sound that is furthest away.

- *Puppet master:* This is another exercise that requires your children to listen very carefully to what is being said and also to block out any distractions. The children work in pairs, one playing the puppet master, the other the puppet. The puppet must shut his or her eyes. The puppet master then walks the puppet around the room, simply by giving verbal instructions, such as *'Take 3 steps forward'* and *'Make a quarter turn to the right'*. The instructions need to be given quietly, so that the individual children can concentrate solely on what their own partners are saying. It's important for the teacher to ensure that the noise levels do not become too high, as this will tend to indicate a loss of focus, and will make the exercise difficult for the children to do safely. When using 'blind' exercises in this way, I always make an absolute rule that anyone doing anything silly or dangerous will have to sit out. After the first time of being sidelined, the children quickly realize that they must take the work seriously, considering the safety of their partners at all times. Again, if you feel uncomfortable with the whole class working at once, simply divide the class in half and get one group working as an audience for the rest.

Thinking and children's behaviour

As I mentioned earlier in this chapter, behaviour is linked fundamentally with thinking skills. A class with poor behaviour is likely to be distracted, and is unlikely to undertake any high quality thinking. A class that can behave well, and a classroom in which the atmosphere is calm and purposeful, will obviously be more effective when it comes to developing individual and group thinking skills. As you will see below, we can actually use our children's thinking skills when trying to work on their behaviour. Our aim should be to persuade them to spend some time thinking about why they behave as they do, about what good behaviour is, and why behaving well is so important.

Here are just a few useful tips about how you can encourage better behaviour from your students, and as a result receive better quality thinking work. For more detailed ideas and advice, see my books *Getting the Buggers to Behave 2* and *Sue Cowley's Teaching Clinic.*

- *Train them up:* I'm a great believer in training my children in the ways in which I want them to behave. It is no use at all expecting 'good' behaviour unless your children are taught exactly what you mean by behaving well. For instance, you might train them in the art of focus, using the exercises described earlier in this chapter. You might also train them in appropriate learning behaviour, such as sitting still while listening, making eye contact with the speaker during discussions, and so on.
- *Make your expectations clear:* The clearer we can make life in the classroom for our children, the better they will behave and consequently the better they will learn. When you first start out with a class, or when you introduce a new activity, such as thinking, take the time to make your expectations clear. A really good way to do this is to use 'I expect' statements. Here are some examples:
  o *'I expect you to listen carefully, and in complete silence, when other people are talking.'*
  o *'I expect you to think about what you're going to say before you speak.'*

    o *'I expect you to take turns to talk when you're working in a group.'*

- *Be a role model for them:* The majority of our students look to us to provide them with a role model of appropriate behaviour. The teacher can also offer a role model of what good thinking actually is. One of the best ways in which you can do this is by making your own thought processes clear and explicit. As you talk with your class about the learning, or about their behaviour, elucidate the thinking processes that are taking place inside your mind, and the reasons behind your thoughts. So you might say: *'I need you all to listen really carefully to these instructions, so that you understand what you have to do, and so that you can complete the work really well.'*

- *Think about behaviour:* When you're hoping to develop thinking skills, it is an excellent idea to spend some time talking with your students about their behaviour – the reasons behind it and why good behaviour is so important. You might use this approach as a whole class activity, aimed specifically at developing thinking skills. You should also aim to get individual students thinking about their behaviour, particularly when they are not behaving as you wish and you have to sanction them. Here are some questions that you might use to focus your discussion.

    o *'Why do people behave as they do?'*
    o *'What is good/bad behaviour?'*
    o *'Why do some students behave well, and others behave badly?'*
    o *'What should we do with children who don't behave well?'*
    o *'Why did you misbehave on this occasion?'*
    o *'What type of sanction or punishment do you deserve?'*
    o *'How can I get you to behave better in the future?'*
    o *'Why is good behaviour so important in the classroom?'*
    o *'What would happen if everyone behaved as they wanted at school, with no rules or sanctions to control them?'*
    o *'What would happen if everyone behaved exactly as they wanted in the world outside of school?'*

3

Planning and teaching thinking

There are two main schools of thought when it comes to incorporating thinking activities into lessons. Some believe that it is best to view thinking as a separate, discrete subject, and to focus exclusively on the teaching of thinking skills outside of the normal curriculum. I would tend to side with the other viewpoint – that the explicit use of thinking skills should be incorporated into every single lesson that you teach. After all, getting our children to learn in the most efficient way is all about encouraging the use of good quality thinking skills. They might be developing an argument, working out how to memorize some facts, applying their reasoning skills to help them solve a puzzle, and so on. All these skills can be put to good use in a whole variety of different lessons and subject areas.

My advice would be to view your lesson planning as a chance to see how many different thinking skills you can incorporate into the work. In this chapter you will find lots of ideas about how to do this. I give some suggestions about how and when to include thinking activities, and I also suggest a range of unusual and engaging exercises to encourage your children to work with and develop their thoughts.

Incorporating thinking activities into lessons

There are lots of opportunities for including thinking activities in your lessons. This applies right across the curriculum and also whether you're working at primary or secondary level. View your lessons as a voyage of discovery, both for the class as a whole, and for the individuals within the group. Although you will clearly be passing on information about a topic, or teaching the children new skills, there should also be an emphasis on allowing the students to discover some of the learning for themselves. Your aim should be to find out what the children already know or think, as well as actually telling them about the topic. Here are some suggestions about how you can use thinking skills within the different parts of your lessons – the beginning, the middle section, and the end.

- *Starting out:* The opening of a lesson is a very good place to incorporate thinking skills. The tendency might be for the teacher to present new ideas to the class right at the start of the lesson, by way of an introduction to the topic. However, consider whether it would be better to get the children thinking for themselves about what they already know. This might take the form of a brainstorm, with the whole class working together to write ideas on the board. Alternatively you might ask individuals or small groups to note their own ideas down on paper and then share these with the class as a whole. In this way you'll be able to find out what your children already know, or think, about a subject, what their preconceptions about the topic are, and whether you already have any 'experts' on this particular subject within the class.

- *Dividing the lesson up:* Learning is most effective when the teacher divides the lesson up into smaller parts with a short break between the different activities. This is important because of the limited concentration span of the average person. We tend to remember most from the start and end of a period of learning, and by breaking up your lesson into a series of parts you can use this aspect of the way in which learning works best. Thinking activities provide a really useful format for giving your class mini breaks within a lesson. You might choose to use purely mental tasks, or ones that require a combination of thought and physical movement. These 'brain gym' exercises are also great fun and can create a very positive atmosphere for learning. Here are some ideas.

o *Mental activities:* To exercise the brain, and to give it a break from a long period of concentrated work, you might try some short mental tasks. For instance, a few quick examples of mental arithmetic, or an anagram written on the board for the children to work out.

o *Physical activities:* Having a brief physical break is an excellent way of refreshing the class, so that the students return to work in a more focused frame of mind. To give just one example, ask your children to put their right hand on the left side of their nose, and the left hand on the right cheek, and then swap the two hands over. Start the exercise off slowly, gradually getting faster and faster.

o *Spoken activities:* If you've been working on a task that requires silent concentration, then a quick burst of focused speaking can work wonders for giving the class a breather. For instance, you might get the children repeating a tongue twister over and over again, such as *'She sells sea shells on the seashore'*. Alternatively, you might use the 'word tennis' exercise described in Chapter 4.

- *Finishing off:* The idea of a plenary at the end of each lesson is not exactly a new one, but it does provide a very useful way of drawing the class together and reviewing the work that has taken place. It is, of course, very important to encourage our children to review and evaluate their own learning, as it helps them to see what has gone well, and also how they might improve in the future. Many thinking skills can be used and developed by incorporating these activities into the end section of your lessons. This might take the form of a whole class activity, or it could be done by individuals or in small groups. Here are some questions to guide your discussion.

o *'What new things have we learnt today?'*
o *'What did you think about this new subject?'*
o *'How well did you complete the tasks?'*
o *'What could you have done better?'*
o *'How could we continue working on this topic?'*
o *'What might I be planning to do next lesson?'*
o *'Who can think of an appropriate homework task?'*

Strategies for teaching children to think

There are literally hundreds of different strategies that you can use in teaching your children how to think. I cover several different ideas below that should help you in your planning of thinking activities, and you'll find lots more tips throughout this book. I would also recommend that you look at some of Edward de Bono's many books on thinking, which give a wide variety of strategies and approaches that you could put to good use in the classroom.

- *Consider the key questions:* Whatever the topic you are teaching, it is well worth having a list of key questions that you might ask the children during the lesson. These key questions should be designed to encourage the students to explore the main ideas of a particular subject area – the 'meat' of the topic, so to speak. Having a written list of these key questions will ensure that you cover all the aspects of the topic that you wish to address. You might also ask your children to come up with a list of key questions that they wish to have answered during the course of studying the topic.
- *Work laterally:* It is very tempting to see thinking as a linear process, in which one thought leads directly on to another. However, many of the 'best' or most interesting thoughts will occur when we take a lateral or sideways approach to our thinking. You can find more information about lateral thinking in Chapter 7. To give a quick example, using a question that starts with the phrase *'But what if . . .'* will help you encourage lateral thought. In a lesson where the children are studying a map to work out where some hidden pirate treasure could be buried, the teacher might intervene to encourage lateral thought by asking *'But what if the treasure is dangerous, what if it was hidden so that nobody could let this danger loose?'*
- *Look at all sides:* Try to encourage your children to think around a subject by looking at it from all sides. You could use the image of a multicoloured box in order to explain this approach to your class. Standing at one side of the box, we might see only red, and this would lead us to assume that the whole box is in fact red.

However, standing on another side we see blue, another green, and so on. This metaphor demonstrates how important it is to try to look at all sides of an issue and to view the situation as a whole, taking an overview before we come to any conclusions.

- *Take a number of different viewpoints:* The thoughts that we come up with will vary a great deal depending on where we stand in relation to an issue, problem or other point in question. Our viewpoint will change according to who we are, what we believe, and so on. Using the metaphor of a box as given above, different people or creatures might see the box in very different ways. To an ant the box would look enormous, a huge tower that blocks out the sun. To a person, the box might be of interest because of what could potentially be inside. And to an elephant the box would seem minuscule, a fragile thing that could be crushed with one single step. Encourage your children to step outside of their own opinions and responses, and to consider the issues you raise from a number of different viewpoints. You might use the 'in role' approach described below to help them do this.

- *Use in role approaches:* When you're aiming to get your children to consider different viewpoints, it's a great idea to get them working in role. By playing a variety of characters, and examining the different responses of each one, they will learn how to think all around a subject. For instance, you might set the class a question about fox hunting, asking *'Should fox hunting be banned?'* Instead of hearing the students' actual viewpoints, if you get them working in role they will be forced to consider what other people (and indeed other creatures) might think. So it is that the children might respond as:

  o *a farmer* who believes that foxes are vermin, and that hunting them is a good way of controlling them;
  o *an animal lover* who feels that hunting is completely unnecessary, and that it is cruel and inhumane;
  o *a member of the hunt* who enjoys the sport and feels that no one else has the right to prevent him from taking part;
  o *a fox* who is terrified of being chased by a pack of dogs, and who (for obvious reasons) doesn't want to get caught and torn apart.

Creating a climate for thinking

As we saw in the previous chapter, it is up to the teacher to encourage the appropriate climate for thought within his or her classroom. We need our children to show the high concentration and good behaviour necessary for quality thinking. We can also go further in creating an environment that both encourages and stimulates thought. When you are planning your lessons, and looking at including thinking skills within the work, consider the following points about creating a suitable climate for thinking.

- *The environment:* The environment provided in our classrooms will have an effect on the quality of thought that occurs. This applies both to the actual physical environment, and also to the way in which we encourage our children to approach the work. For instance, in a noisy and overexcited atmosphere, it will prove difficult for the class to concentrate hard and think properly. Most of the time your aim should be to offer your children a calm, quiet, restful space in which to consider their thoughts (although, of course, there will be occasions when you need and want a loud and energetic feeling in the room). If the physical constraints of your classroom allow it, do try to ensure that the students have sufficient space within which to work. This might mean that you have to think carefully about the way that you arrange the desks within the room.
- *Sensory stimulus:* Stimulating all the senses can play a crucial part in creating a suitable atmosphere for thinking. Consider how you can do this within your own classroom when planning thinking activities. For instance, you might bring in some different scents, perhaps a selection of leaves from herbal plants. The children could then be blindfolded and asked to smell the different herbs in turn. Music can offer us an excellent backdrop for developing thinking and can have an influence on the type of atmosphere that is created within your room. Consider, too, what your children see within your room – are the displays bright and interesting, is the room tidy and well organized? All these sensory issues will affect the thinking that takes place.

- *Inspirations for the lesson:* Props, objects and other 'dramatic' approaches can offer a powerful inspiration for our children's thought. These dramatic ideas could include the use of different lighting, sound and special effects, and so on. To give an example, you might decide to use some unusual items to spark off a piece of creative writing. You could bring in a handbag containing objects such as a computer disk, a map, a Bible, a card with a name and number on it, and so on. From these items the children could start to build a character, working as detectives to try and figure out who the bag belongs to.
- *The teacher's approach:* The way that you as a teacher actually run your lessons will also help create a climate for thinking. Aim to make the process of thinking within the lesson as explicit as possible, taking the time to talk about exactly what is going on inside your brain and also those of your children. Try to encourage diverse and interesting thought by responding in a very positive way to unusual suggestions. If you can allow your class the freedom to take the lesson in the direction that they wish, this will also help to stimulate lateral and creative thinking. It can feel rather nerve-racking at first to divert from your lesson plan (and from the tight structure of much of the curriculum), but it will in fact pay dividends in the long run in terms of the impact on your children's learning.

Formats for thinking

As with all learning, some of the best thinking work will take place where the teacher provides a clear and engaging format for the children to use. Of course, one approach is simply to say *'Let's think about this question/issue/puzzle'*, and divide the students up into discussion groups. Alternatively, you might lead a whole class discussion on a particular topic. However, if you give the children an interesting format with which to structure their thinking, they are far more likely to display high levels of motivation, and to focus fully on the work. When you are planning your lessons, try to use the technique of lateral thinking (described in Chapter 7) to explore how you might approach a particular topic area through an interesting and engaging format.

What exactly, then, do I mean by an 'interesting format' for thinking? To give an example, the students that we teach live very much within a television culture. The sensible teacher can take advantage of this by using some familiar television formats to help structure exercises that encourage thinking. You can find a couple of ideas below to help you get started. You'll also see a description of a drama format known as 'The role of the expert', which can be used to start the children working in role and utilizing thinking skills within any area of the curriculum.

Countdown

On this television programme the contestants work with letters and numbers to find words and mathematical solutions. This format could prove a really fun way to start your class doing some thinking work in either English or maths. The programme pits two contestants against each other to see who can do best in the activities as described below. One of the presenters is Carol Vorderman, a personality of whom your class will probably already be aware. Here are a few tips and pointers to help you organize yourself.

- Rather than working with two individuals, use the same format to set the tasks for your whole class to complete. See who can work out the longest word, or the correct mathematical formula, as described below.
- Set the game up as a competition, using the relevant vocabulary, such as 'contestants', 'winner', and so on. This will help engage the class, making the activities a challenge that they will be keen to complete.
- If possible, give rewards for those who do well in the game, although ensure that you also encourage those students who find the exercises hard to complete.
- An excellent reward and motivator (for good work, behaviour or concentration) is to pick an individual to play 'Carol', or a group of children to act as the 'checkers'.

- Give the students a short time limit within which to work to ensure that they maintain a sense of urgency. (On the programme this is a minute, but you might like to give your children two minutes so that they have a little more time to think.)
- Use a timer, if possible a big clock with a second hand as they do on the television programme. You might even tape-record the ticking 'countdown' music to make the scenario more realistic.
- Make the way that the activities are structured very similar to the actual television programme. This will help ensure that your students are fully engaged and excited to get going.
- You might like to show a clip from the television programme itself, to help enthuse your children, and also to show them how the format works.
- After you have tried this activity a couple of times, spend some time exploring possible thinking approaches and techniques that will enable your children to do better. Encourage those who find the exercises easiest to examine the thinking processes they have used to do well. This will help them achieve metacognition (awareness of their own thought processes).
- Some variations on the game include giving the children a dictionary each to help them find words, allowing the students to use calculators for the maths exercises, and putting the class into small groups to work together on the tasks.

Here's an explanation of the game, to show you how it works. I also describe the various organizational aspects that the teacher will need to undertake to use *Countdown* in the classroom. You'll find a list of the benefits involved in the different exercises, how the work will develop thinking skills, and also some other subject-specific areas that it develops.

Word hunt

- Write out the letters of the alphabet on large pieces of card. Depending on the age of your children you might include more of certain letters to make the exercise easier (for instance, I would nominate 's', 'a', 'e', 't' and 'd').

- Put the letters face down on a table. Organize a space on the wall where the letters can be pasted up, and have a supply of Blu-tack available to do this.
- Ask for a volunteer to play the part of Carol Vorderman and pick up and paste the letters as chosen (see below).
- Ask for a team of students to act as 'checkers' at the end of the game (again, see below for their role). Give the checkers a dictionary to use when the activity is finished.
- Ask the students to raise their hands if they wish to pick a letter. They must ask for either a vowel or a consonant. Depending on the age of your children you might take the opportunity to introduce these terms to the class, or spend a short while clarifying what they mean.
- Ask 'Carol' to choose a 'picker' to nominate a letter. 'Carol' then picks up each letter and sticks it on the wall, until you have the required amount. Around eight letters is a good number, as used on the programme. However, you might allow the class to pick out more at first, to make the exercise easier.
- Encourage the children to select a good mixture of vowels and consonants, as this will make it possible for them to find more words. (If on the first attempt they pick only vowels or consonants, you might like to let them try this, so that they see how it makes the game impossible!)
- Once the letters are picked, give the class a signal that the time is starting. You might use a bell or perhaps say *'Ready, steady, go'*.
- The children then have a set period of time in which to find the longest word possible using these letters. Each letter can only be used once, but the letters can be placed in any order. Encourage the class to keep looking for the entire time, and not to settle for the first word that is found. (You might like to take the chance to explore how words can be lengthened by adding endings such as 's', 'es', 'ed' or 'ing'.)
- When the time is up, ask the children to raise their hands if they have an eight-letter word, a seven-letter word, a six-letter word, and so on, until you find the child with the longest word.
- When a winner or winners is found, ask your team of checkers to verify the word, ensuring that it is in the dictionary, and that it is spelt correctly.

This game has a number of different benefits, not only in the area of thinking skills, but also when it comes to developing other aspects of writing and spelling. Some of these benefits are listed below:

- Seeing and exploring patterns within our language.
- Exploring different letter combinations, particularly those that appear in many words in the English language.
- Experimenting with different letter orders to find the longest possible word.
- Looking at ways in which we can change words so that they become longer. For example, this might be through changes of tense, such as adding 'ed', or through creating plurals, adding 's' and 'es'.
- Work on vowels and consonants: what they are and how they work together.

Sum hunt
In the maths section of the game, the contestants pick six numbers. These numbers are designated either large (20, 25, 50, 100, and so forth) or small (1–10). A total is then chosen at random (on the television programme this is done by a machine), for instance, 397. The challenge is to put the small and large numbers together in such a way that they make a sum whose total is the same as the random number chosen by the machine. Each number can only be used once, although not all the numbers have to be used within the calculation. The winner is the contestant who is closest to the correct number.

So, to show you how this works, the numbers that have been picked might be:

$$5 \ 3 \ 7 \ 10 \ 25 \ 70$$

With a total to be achieved of 397, the calculation might go as follows:

$5 \times 7 = 35$
$35 \times 10 = 350$

$350 + \mathbf{70} = 420$

$420 - \mathbf{25} = 395$

$395 + \mathbf{3} = 398$ (1 away from the total required)

Here's a brief explanation of how to organize the game so that you can use it in your classroom.

- Make cards containing numbers. Divide these numbers up into 'small' numbers (1 to 10) and 'big' numbers (for instance, 20, 35, 50, 100).
- Again, a volunteer works as 'Carol' and asks the class to select some numbers (around six numbers will work well). It is up to the children whether they choose several small and only one big number, a mixture, or just one small number and a lot of big ones. You might decide to do some discussion work on which approach is best, bringing out the thinking involved in making this decision.
- Now pick a random number that the children have to reach with their calculation. You might simply have some random numbers written on cards, which you could place in a bag and ask the children to draw out. Alternatively, you might ask for a volunteer to choose a number.
- Give the class a short period of time in which to make a calculation that gets them as close as possible to the random number. Around 1–2 minutes should be about right.
- Check to see whether anybody has the exact number or, if not, to see who has come closest. The winner should then come up to the front to write his or her calculation up on the board.

Rikki Lake

In recent years, American TV shows such as *Oprah, Jerry Springer* and *Rikki Lake* have become extremely popular both in the USA and in the UK. For those of you who haven't seen this type of show, the basic format is that of a chat show but with a difference. Ordinary people with extraordinary problems and experiences come onto the show to talk about what they've been through. Often, these people will reveal an issue or problem for the first time, in front of the television cameras. For instance, on a show dealing with bigamy, you might meet a woman who doesn't realize that her husband has actually been married before (and never divorced). During the show, the revelation is made, and the reactions can be understandably extreme. The presenter talks with the guests about their experiences, usually with the aim of trying to resolve the problems (at least to some extent). The audience are also invited to make comments about the issues raised. Frequently, the discussions become extremely heated and bouncers have to intervene physically between the parties involved.

These shows offer the teacher an interesting format within which to discuss some really powerful issues. It proves particularly useful for work that requires a debate of some sort. You might use it to explore a number of different moral or personal, social and health education (PSHE) issues. There are a number of points in favour of using this type of format, not least the way in which it engages and enthuses the children. You will find that your class quickly starts working within the 'rules' of the format (most of them will already know it well). You will also discover that the students get really involved in putting points for and against the subject of debate. Below is just one suggestion to get you started.

'My teen is out of control'

Parents of 'out-of-control' teenagers come on the show to complain about their children's behaviour. The teens are given the right of reply, and the audience give their own views about whether the parents or children are in the right. Points are made and discussed about the use of curfews, sanctions, the dangers of being out late at night, and so on.

The role of the expert

The 'role of the expert' is a technique used within drama lessons, but it is also a format that lends itself very well to the teaching of thinking skills right across the curriculum. The basic idea behind the technique is that the students get into role as a character, playing experts on a particular topic or area. They then work in this role for an extended period of time, undertaking tasks that the expert would do, solving problems that are set for them, and generally behaving and working in the guise of this person. By using the role of the expert, students can develop various different areas of their thinking. These include:

- independent thought;
- group discussion;
- understanding and empathy;
- problem solving;
- logic and reasoning;
- forward planning.

The role of the expert can be used with a number of different structures: you might have individuals working alone, you might use group work or even approach the tasks as a whole class. The technique has a number of great benefits in the classroom.

- Once they get into character, the students tend to take a very mature approach to the tasks set, and will often extend the work beyond what you might expect.
- In my experience, children love the chance to play someone else and enjoy the opportunity of going along with the fiction that the teacher has created.
- The enjoyment factor in the learning means that motivation is generally very high and the children work with enthusiasm and commitment.
- If there is any off-task behaviour, the teacher can easily move the children back onto task by reminding them about how their character would behave in 'real life'.
- The learning that takes place can be via the research required for playing the part and also by discovery through actually 'living' the role.
- The exercise provides very memorable and enjoyable lessons for the children, and consequently behaviour tends to be good and learning is of a high quality.
- The role of the expert can be adapted and applied to a whole host of different subjects, as you will see from the sample lesson

that I give below. As well as being applicable across the curriculum, this type of work is also very good for combining skills from several different subject areas.

At first, it can feel a little strange for non-drama teachers to be using a fictional approach in their lessons. You may also be a little concerned about how your students will react, and whether you will be able to control their responses. There really is no need to worry – once you start the activities you will find that the children quickly begin to take responsibility for their own work and behaviour. Here are some tips that will help you in using the role of the expert within your classroom.

- *Play a part yourself:* It is a very good idea for the teacher to take an active part in the fiction. Introduce the scenario in role (see the point below), and maintain this role throughout your time working on the project. This will enable you to work from within the story that is created and allow you to control and direct the scenario (and the children's work) as it develops.
- *Don't explain the fiction:* When you first introduce this exercise, it works really well if you do this by going straight into character rather than explaining what the lesson is going to be about. At first, you may find that your students are a little puzzled and that they ask you *'Sir/Miss, what's going on?'* However, if you persevere you will soon find that the children pick up on what is happening. The key is to refuse to respond as a teacher, and simply continue your explanation in role.
- *Make use of props:* As I've already pointed out, props or objects can be a very powerful motivation and inspiration within the classroom setting. In the role of the expert they are particularly useful when you are first introducing the scenario, as they give the children a 'hook' that helps them to focus, motivates them, and moves them seamlessly into the fiction. In the sample lesson given below, the prop is a letter asking for help.
- *Make use of special effects:* As well as using props, it is a great idea to include other dramatic effects to help you engage the children and pull them into the whole idea of the fiction. You

might use a tape of bird song to create a background atmosphere when working on a rainforest theme. You could darken the room and give the children torches if they were working as ghost hunters.

- *Give them structure:* Using the role of the expert does not mean simply giving the children a character and then having a free-for-all to see what is learned. This will generally result in chaos! It is very important for the teacher to structure the way in which the scenario proceeds. As we saw above, this is one very good reason for the teacher to play a role within the story. You might also impose a structure by giving your experts a list of pre-set tasks that they must complete. Alternatively, you might involve the whole class in thinking about and planning the activities that need to be done, perhaps by holding a meeting in which they discuss the issues at hand.

- *Delegate!* I'm a great believer in delegation within the classroom (it makes our job a little easier, and that can't be bad!). The whole point of the role of the expert is that it actually encourages the teacher to do less, and the students to do more. If you have a task that needs completing within the drama, for instance taking notes during a meeting, then make sure you delegate this to one of your experts. Not only will they love taking on these 'adult' tasks, but the more you can encourage the children to do for themselves, the greater the ownership of the learning they will feel, and the more they will develop their thinking.

- *Use the fun to control the class:* I promise you that your students (of whatever age) will find this type of activity great fun, as it offers them something rather different from the usual lessons that they encounter in school. You can use this fact to your advantage when it comes to controlling the class. If the students do look like getting out of hand, there are two options to get them back in line. You might either:
  o re-focus the group from within the fiction, using your character to pull them back together or
  o stop the story completely and talk to the students out of role about how they need to behave if they wish to continue with this work.

To explain this technique further, here is an example of how you might use the role of the expert within your own classroom. By looking at the explanation of this scenario, you should be able to work out ways in which to use the approach in all different areas of the curriculum.

The disaster relief team

Curriculum area: geography.
Cross-curricular links: English, drama, art, science.
Props and resources: letter from the team asking for help; books and computers for research.

The children work as a team of disaster relief experts, going into an area where there has been a natural disaster to help the local people. Depending on the type of geographical phenomenon you wish to study, you might set up a scenario where there has been a volcanic eruption, an earthquake, a flood, a drought, and so on. An excellent way to introduce the fiction is to write a letter asking for help, which has (supposedly) been written by the people of the village where the disaster struck. Here are some ideas about the tasks that you might use with your experts.

- *Whole class meeting:* After introducing the scenario, a good first step would be to spend some time talking as a whole class (in role). Your students could come up with a list of tasks that need to be completed before they set out, such as researching the phenomenon in question, finding out more about the area where the disaster has occurred, making lists of and packing the relevant equipment (medical supplies, search equipment, irrigation machinery, and so forth), deciding on travel arrangements, making arrangements for search dogs to come with you, and so on.
- *Research:* Again working in role, your experts could spend some time doing detailed research of the specific problem that the village has experienced. This might involve reading in the library, looking for information on the Internet, quizzing other experts (getting you to tell them what you know), writing to

organizations experienced in dealing with these types of problems, contacting the local tourist board for this geographical area, and so on.

- *The journey:* Although not strictly speaking 'geography', it can be a very good idea to dramatize the journey to the area where the disaster has occurred. This helps to make the whole scenario more effective and is also great fun for the children. If you are travelling by aeroplane you might ask the class to make tickets and ask for volunteers to act as cabin crew, the pilot, and so on. Once the plane lands, it could be that you have to travel across rough and dangerous terrain, perhaps encountering physical dangers such as wild animals. To dramatize this part of the journey in the classroom you could split your class up into small groups and ask them to plan a short scene in which they come across danger of some type. These scenes could then be shown to the class.

- *Arrival:* Once they 'arrive' at their destination, it is a good idea to have another whole class meeting. At this meeting you can come up with a list of tasks to be completed, asking your experts to split themselves up into groups in order to complete the necessary jobs. For instance, if you were studying the impact of drought on the village, these jobs could include:
  o writing a report on the reasons behind the failure of this year's crops;
  o making a plan of the village to show the areas where crops could best be grown;
  o planning an irrigation system to keep the crops watered in the future;
  o organizing equipment, medical aid and food supplies;
  o if available, using an area of the school gardens to grow some different food crops to test which are most and least susceptible to drought.

Thinking and the National Curriculum

Thinking skills have now been given a section of their own within the National Curriculum. This reflects an understanding of how

important is it that our students know *how* to learn, as well
to learn. On the National Curriculum website, *www.nc.uk.net*, you
can find ideas and resources for incorporating thinking skills right
across the school. To give a very brief overview, the National
Curriculum divides thinking skills into five different areas. These are:

- information processing;
- reasoning;
- enquiry;
- creativity;
- evaluation.

Various skills can be identified within these different areas. For
instance, within the information processing component the children might be working with information in various ways. These
are identified as:

- finding relevant information;
- organizing information;
- comparing and contrasting information;
- identifying and analysing relationships.

The National Curriculum website allows you to search for
thinking skills in different curriculum areas, and at all the different Key Stages. So, the science teacher might make a search to see
how he or she can 'develop evaluation criteria' at Key Stage 3.

Making thinking visible

As I noted earlier, one of the difficulties with teaching (and particularly with assessing) thinking skills is that thought is an invisible area of learning. We have no way of seeing exactly what is
going on in our children's heads when we set them a thinking
task. Consequently, when we are planning the teaching of thinking skills we need to consider how we might find concrete ways
of viewing the learning that is taking place. This will help us to
judge whether our methods are working to their best advantage

and it will also allow us to assess how well each child is doing in the development of his or her thinking. There are two main possibilities when it comes to making thinking visible: we either 'see' it through hearing what our children have to say, or we see it literally when it is written down on the page, or noted in some other visual format.

Seeing thinking verbally

- *Thinking out loud:* When thought processes take place verbally, the teacher is able to hear the thinking that is going on, and consequently to make some judgements about the type and quality of this thought. The teacher should take into account the fact that there may be a gap between what our children are actually thinking and their ability to verbalize this process. In order to 'see' thinking orally you might use:
  o whole-class discussions;
  o group discussions;
  o paired discussions;
  o individual, paired or group presentations;
  o class assemblies.
- *Tape recording:* Using a tape recorder to make a record of our children's thinking has a number of advantages, not least the fact that it gives us permanent evidence of what their thoughts were at a particular moment in time. We might simply use a tape recorder to catch a short piece of group or class discussion. Alternatively, we could ask the students to actually plan what is to be said, for instance, in a radio programme on a particular topic. The many other benefits of using tape recording include the following:
  o it provides an excellent way of motivating and enthusing the class in their thinking work;
  o it can be very instructive for the students to get a chance to hear what they sound like: the way that they speak, what they actually talk about, and also the way that they structure their ideas;
  o the process of making a recording will develop various skills, such as pre-planning, if the piece is to be planned or scripted;

o taping also offers the chance to practise editing of thoughts or ideas, through the use of taping, listening and re-taping.

- *Video:* Making a video offers many of the benefits listed above for tape recording. In addition, of course, seeing a video of their work allows the students to look at the way they use body language, gesture, and so on. In my experience, students absolutely love the idea of making and seeing a video of themselves in action. Again, the videotape provides the teacher with a permanent record of his or her children's work.

Seeing thinking visually

- *Brainstorming:* When thinking is recorded visually on paper, we can see at least some of the processes that are taking place in our children's minds. Brainstorming (see Chapter 4) has a huge range of other benefits, perhaps one of the most important of which is that it helps teach our children to structure their ideas and thought processes. Putting thoughts onto paper, as with all the other suggestions below, again gives the teacher a permanent record of the children's thinking.

- *Turning thoughts into images:* As well as using the written word, we can also use pictures and images with our children to help both them and us visualize the thinking that takes place in their brains. There are a number of different possibilities for the use of images. These include:
  o making a drawing which includes lots of different images to represent a number of diverse thoughts on a topic;
  o creating a single image, perhaps a symbolic one, that 'stands for' and sums up their thinking on a particular topic or issue;
  o using quick doodles to note down their thoughts, perhaps during a verbal presentation to the class;
  o creating collages by using cut-out images from magazines. (This approach is especially useful where the children do not have sufficient artistic skills to record their thoughts as they would wish.)

- *Diagrams:* Diagrams provide a very useful visual way of representing and noting down thinking processes. The use of arrows, lines, circles and other diagrammatic symbols allows us to add further layers of meaning to the image. For instance, we might show connections between ideas using arrows, or we could circle a word to show that it is particularly important. When creating diagrams, you can also encourage your children to use colour to help them differentiate and develop the different thoughts.

Assessing thinking

As we saw above ('Making thinking visible'), it is vital for the teacher to be able to *see* the thinking that is going on in some form or another. One of the reasons why we might want to do this is so that we can assess the work. We might also need to have a record of how our children's thought is developing, and keep notes of this development for future reference. Assessing thinking is not easy. How, after all, do you put a value on creativity, originality, individuality, and so on? How, too, do you assess a subject which is not necessarily about right and wrong in the same way that traditional learning is often judged? In some ways, we would be better off not making any formal assessments of our children's thinking skills, and instead letting them just get on with developing their minds the best that they can. Obviously, however, there will be occasions on which you do wish to make some type of formal assessment of your children's thinking skills, and how these are developing.

The National Curriculum offers us various levels within different curriculum areas that can help us in assessing our children's thinking. A search of the National Curriculum website (*www.nc.uk.net*) will help you to isolate the components of a specific subject area that particularly relate to thinking skills. You could then use these to help inform your assessment.

Alternatively, you might decide to develop your own criteria for assessing your students' thinking skills. To give just one example of how this might be done, let's say you had decided to focus on how well your students were able to argue or debate their own stance on a particular issue. To obtain some idea of who is working at what standard, you might come up with several different skill identifiers within this specific area of thought. These could include:

- makes statements that show an opinion;
- makes statements that show a well-informed opinion;
- backs statements up with relevant arguments or evidence;
- is able to take lateral jumps in thought to show other important factors;
- is able to understand different viewpoints, and argue from any standpoint.

4

Structuring thinking

Because of its nebulous and individualistic nature, it is tempting to believe that thinking can take place without any kind of structure at all. Of course, this is entirely true on one level – there is certainly no harm at all in simply allowing the mind to wander, to see where our thoughts might take us. This type of thinking is one very valuable way of exercising our minds and it can certainly free us up to find new ideas or fresh approaches. However, for some (perhaps many) of our students, asking them to think without giving them a structure within which to work will simply result in a lack of quality thought. Consequently, when you introduce the majority of thinking activities, it is important that you give your children a structured and well-planned system within which to do the thinking.

In this chapter you will find lots of ideas for different ways in which you might structure your children's thought. As you'll see, the 'structures' include some very free approaches, and also some very tightly constructed exercises. Which ones you choose depends very much on the type of work you are doing, although do not be afraid to use one of the free approaches within a traditionally tightly structured lesson or activity. I also include a section in this chapter that gives lots of thoughts and tips about structuring both discussion and group work.

Structures for thinking

Our brains work by seeing and creating patterns that allow us to order our thinking. By making connections between what we see, what we know and what we have discovered, we are able to give a structure to the world in which we live. Structures allow us to put down patterns and give shape to what is inside our heads. The ability to organize our thoughts plays an important role in the development of higher-order thinking skills. Below you'll find some ideas and tips about using a whole host of different structures. These range from typically visual structures, such as brainstorming and free association, to structures for spoken thought, such as circle time.

Brainstorming

The brainstorm is the teacher's familiar old friend. In fact, it's so familiar to most of us that perhaps we use it without thinking properly about how and why it works. The brainstorm comes in various guises and is also known as the scattergram or spidergram. The majority of us would probably use a brainstorm when starting off with a new topic. We might ask the children to work individually, writing a word in the centre of the page, then noting down all the things that they already know about the subject. Alternatively, we might work as a whole class, noting the ideas that are given on the board.

The great thing about the brainstorm is that it allows us to take a very clear overview of where we are with a particular subject area. Because the nature of the brainstorm is very much diagrammatic, it helps us to structure our thoughts and see what connections could be made between the different ideas. When using brainstorming with your children, it is worth spending some time trying out new or different approaches. Here are some thoughts on how you can use brainstorms in a fresh and innovative way.

- *Make the brainstorm visually interesting:* Rather than simply asking your children to draw the classic spidergram, why not start them off with a slightly more inspiring (i.e. gruesome) picture of a brain exploding on the page? By making the brainstorm format visually interesting you will engage your students' interest and attention.

- *Use colours:* A brainstorm allows us to structure our thoughts through the way that we place them on the page. An excellent way to develop this idea is to add in the use of colour. When brainstorming, try asking your students to use colours to differentiate between different ideas and thoughts. They might do this while writing the initial brainstorm, or they might work out a draft first in black and white, and then rewrite it using colours. Doing this is a fairly intuitive process for most of us. For instance, we might use the colour blue to indicate calm thoughts, or thoughts somehow linked to water. Similarly, the colour red is traditionally associated with passion, heat, fire; the colour yellow with sunshine and happiness; the colour green with nature, and so on. Some very interesting thinking could take place during the process of deciding on the relevant colours for different ideas. The children will have to use the skill of classifying and sorting, as well as approaching the work in a creative and intuitive way.

- *Use images and symbols:* We do tend to think of brainstorms as being made up of language – a series of words written down on the page in the familiar brainstorm format. However, you could try getting your children to create brainstorms that are made up of images or symbols instead. Again, the skills that are used during the process of deciding what images or symbols to use will help your children develop their thinking further.

- *Use different materials:* Taking this idea further, why not use a range of different materials to create your visual brainstorms? For instance, this might involve giving the children magazines or other pictures so that they can create a collage brainstorm.

- *Make it big!* In my experience, you can make a great impact with your children by using size as a factor in their work. You might decide to create a huge brainstorm by going outside into the playground with your class. The children could then work together to draw different parts of a huge brainstorm in chalk on the playground floor.

- *Use it for a range of purposes:* Although we would normally use a brainstorm as the initial working document on a new topic, in fact they have a wide range of potential uses. These uses include:

o *Planning:* Brainstorms offer an excellent format for planning many different types of work. For instance, the different sections of a brainstorm could be used to develop a selection of ideas for a story. In exams, a quick series of brainstorms will help the students plan their work before they start.

o *Essay writing:* When writing a lengthy essay, I would always recommend the use of a number of brainstorms. Each brief brainstorm can correlate with a single paragraph of the essay, with a single idea and its development contained within each one. These 'planning brainstorms' are more fully explained in my book *Getting the Buggers to Write*.

o *Revision:* Revising via a series of brainstorms offers an excellent way of condensing information, and also of putting things into an appropriate order. The students can then decide upon a way of remembering the words at the centre of each brainstorm. These words act as reminders to jolt their memories when it comes to exam time. For some thoughts about how to memorize these words see Chapter 5, which deals with memory.

Free association

Free association shares some similarities with brainstorming, but it requires the children to take a different approach in their thinking. Rather than noting down all the facts or points that they already know about a subject, when using free association they are encouraged to take a much more creative approach. Free association is less about linear and structured thinking and much more about lateral ideas and intuitive connections. Basically, when you free associate you allow your mind to wander, to see where your thoughts might lead you.

There are a number of different ways in which you can use free association in the classroom. Perhaps the most obvious approach is to use the written free association, in which you start the class off with a word ('Light' in the example given in Figure 4.1 on page 71) and they then write down all the words and ideas that spring to mind. The process of free association is designed to encourage the children to make lateral connections and to take a very individualized approach to their thinking. It is useful for a whole variety of subject areas, but perhaps particularly so for the more creative topics. For instance, you might use it as a starting point when writing stories or poetry.

Free association does not necessarily have to be done by writing words on paper. As well as creating written free associations, you might also like to try the drawn and spoken free association activities described below. Here are some useful tips for working on free association with your class.

- *Set the boundaries:* Although the aim of the exercise is to allow free thought, it is still a good idea to give a time limit: 'free' does not necessarily mean having a completely unspecified range within which to work. By setting a boundary for your children, you will help motivate them by giving them a target for which to aim. You will also encourage them to think in a focused way.
- *Work fast and furious:* Carrying on from the point above, it is useful to make the class work within quite a short time span and to keep writing as quickly as possible for the whole of the time given. This helps prevent the brain from intervening and editing out any thoughts that do not seem to be relevant. By doing this you help your children to include some of the more interesting thoughts that might occur to them, but which they might feel are irrelevant, and consequently not write down. A good time limit could be about two or three minutes.
- *Make it fun:* Try to find ways of making the whole process fun and exciting. There are a whole host of different ways in which you could do this. I've given just a couple of ideas below, but the only real limit is your imagination!
  - o *Do it to music:* Music can help by giving a specified timeframe within which to work. It will also help to give an inspirational backdrop to the exercise. Depending on the mood you wish to create, or on the type of work you are doing, you might use a calm, slow piece of music to encourage focused thought, or you could use a fast and lively soundtrack to keep the children on track and energized.

o *Use a fun stimulus:* Why not start off your free association by using a prop? This item could act as a fun stimulus for the work, and help the children use the more visual parts of their brains. For instance, a good starting point for thoughts about light could be a candle or a light bulb. The candle would probably take their thoughts in a very different direction to those inspired by the man-made light bulb.

- *Use a structure:* The typical brainstorm structure is one good starting point for free association. In the example given in Figure 4.1, the word 'Light' comes in the centre of the page, with arrows leading off in different directions to show the various links. Some good quality thinking will take place as your children work out how to divide up their ideas by aiming to connect those points which have a common thread. Alternatively, your structure does not necessarily have to be a 'tight' one such as that given by the brainstorm. Instead, you might use the stream of consciousness technique described in Chapter 7.

- *Include everything:* Ask the children to write down everything that comes into their heads, rather than editing their thoughts to start off with. The editing and selection process can then be done later on, after the initial inspiration.

- *Words or phrases:* The children's response does not necessarily have to take the form of single words. Explain to them that it might also include common sayings or other short phrases that spring to mind. In Figure 4.1 the writer includes the book title *Where the Wild Things Are* by making a connection to the fear of the dark.

- *Encourage the 'splatter-gun' effect:* The aim here is literally to 'splatter' thoughts onto the page, in a similar way to the stream of consciousness (see Chapter 7). The quicker they work, the less likely the children will be to edit their thoughts and feelings for fear of being 'wrong' or 'weird'.

- *Associate outwards:* With free association, the thoughts do not necessarily all have to connect to the word at the centre of the page. Show your children how they can also associate outwards, by connecting up their ideas to the previous word or phrase. For instance, in Figure 4.1, the words 'Day and night' spring off into an association with 'Scared of the dark'. The writer has made an emotional link that occurs when she thinks of night time.

- *No right or wrong:* Encourage your students to go off at tangents, and not to be afraid of getting it 'right' or 'wrong'. Remind them that there is no 'correct' answer. All the children in the class will come up with their own response. Although there will probably be similarities in the first few words that are written down, they should then move off at a tangent and explore their own individual thought processes.

- *Use all the senses:* As your children write, you can ask them questions to help develop their thinking. For instance, you might talk about how the senses could relate to the word. Ask questions such as *'What do you see when you think of this word?'* to help them come up with more ideas.

- *Use the emotions:* As well as a sensory response, it is also useful to encourage the children to include emotional reactions to the initial stimulus. For instance, in the example given the writer associates 'Scared of the dark' with the words 'Day and night'.

- *Include questions:* In addition to writing down words or phrases that occur during the free association, your children might also write down questions that crop up in their heads but to which they have no immediate answer. For instance, in Figure 4.1 we can see that the writer asks herself *'What sort of things are heavy?'*, posing a thought that could be worked on later.

- *Edit afterwards:* When the exercise is finished you can use the editing process to develop your children's thinking skills further. You might ask the students to cut down all the associations they have thought of, picking out only the most important or interesting. They might do this by circling the five 'best' words or ideas, or by crossing out any words or ideas that they're not interested in pursuing.

- *Try it drawn:* Using a drawn free association offers an alternative for primary-aged children who do not yet have a wide enough vocabulary to write down all the words that might crop up in their thinking. If you choose to free associate using pictures, ask your students to draw the simplest images that they can find, rather than spending a long time making detailed drawings. Alternatively, you might use the collage idea explained above in the section on brainstorming.

- *Try it spoken:* As another alternative to paper-based free associations, why not try the exercise as a spoken one instead? There are a number of different ways in which you could do this. You might use the 'word tennis' exercise described on p. 81. Alternatively, you could work with the whole class. To do this, get the children standing in a circle. The teacher then starts the exercise with a word (such as 'blue' or 'angry'). The children quickly go around the circle, free associating to add a single word each time.

Circle time

Circle time has become a very popular format for discussion and thinking work, particularly in the primary classroom. The idea is basically that the children sit or stand in a circle and then do some activities as a whole class, working around the circle. This format is most useful for discussion tasks, especially those where the teacher wants the whole class to contribute ideas. Drama teachers, and those of other practical subjects, often use the format of a circle to start their lessons. Although it might require some furniture rearrangement in the secondary school, teachers in other subjects can also use circle time to great effect. There is a whole range of reasons why the structure of a circle is such a useful one in general, and for thinking activities specifically.

- *Everyone can see everyone else:* Working in a circle allows the children to see all of their classmates at once. This means that they can make eye contact with the person speaking. It also encourages good focus on what is being said. And, of course, it means that the teacher can see all the students, and consequently keep an eye on them to make sure that they're all paying attention.
- *Everyone can hear everyone else:* In the traditional classroom layout, there will be occasions when a child speaking at the front of the room cannot be heard by those at the back. In a circle, it is easy for each student to hear what his or her classmates are saying.

- *Democracy:* The circle provides a supremely democratic format for talking exercises. Everyone is able to take their turn, as the activity moves around the circle so that all the students can participate. In many circle activities, the class must act as a unit in order for the work to be successful, and this will help encourage your children's co-operative skills.

- *Symbolism:* The circle is a very powerful symbol. As I pointed out above, it provides a truly democratic approach, symbolically showing that all the participants are equal. This should, in my opinion, include the teacher. He or she can take an active part in the circle time, working alongside the children and providing an excellent role model for them. Symbolically, the circle says: *'We all join together to do the work to the best of our ability'*.

- *A shared experience:* When you use a circle in your classroom, the sense of taking part in a shared activity or experience is very strong. This helps the teacher build up a sense of the class working together, and helps to ensure that everyone contributes equally to the work.

- *Pass it on:* Because of its shape, a circle is excellent for passing around ideas, and joining these ideas up together. It is also very useful for passing round physical items to spark off thinking activities. Here are a couple of suggestions to show you how you can pass on both ideas and items.

    o *Shared story:* In this activity, the children work together to create a story. Each participant says a single word, or a single sentence, going around the circle to develop their story. There are many benefits in this exercise where the area of thinking skills is concerned. The children must listen carefully to what's gone before, or they will not be able to participate. They must also add logically to the story that is being created, rather than simply coming up with ideas of their own that do not follow on with the train of thought.

    o *Shared item:* For this exercise, the children pass round an item, for example, a box. Your discussion might include asking the students what could be in the box, or what it feels like, for example, heavy or light. This can be shown by the way in which the class interacts dramatically with the box (it does not necessarily have to be factually accurate). So, the teacher might show that the box is very heavy, by the way in which he or she holds it, and the children could emulate this as the box is passed around.

As a drama teacher, I use the format of a circle all the time. I start my lessons with the class sat in a circle, to take the register and set the first activity. I also use a circle when I want to demonstrate an exercise to the class, with myself and a volunteer working inside the circle so that everyone can see. Another time when I use a circle is to pull the class back together for reviews or evaluations, for instance, at the end of a lesson or activity. I would highly recommend that you make use of circles too, especially when you are working on thinking skills that involve discussion work with your class. Here are some useful tips for working in this format, garnered from years of circular experience!

- *Get the shape right:* It might sound rather minor and petty, but I always insist that the shape of the circle is right. Rather than a ragged-looking oval shape, I demand that the class sits or stands in a completely circular circle, and I won't begin the lesson or activity until I get what I want. There are a couple of reasons for doing this. First, if the circle is lopsided then you do not get the effect whereby everyone can see everyone else without having to crane their necks. Second, an expectation of a high quality circle is all part of my high expectations of the class.
- *Allow children to 'pass':* One of the dangers with using circles is that the children can feel as though they are 'on the spot', expected to 'produce' in front of all their classmates. For instance, you might use the shared story exercise explained above and find that one child so lacks confidence that he or she freezes and cannot add a word or a sentence. This leads to the rest of the class complaining, and consequently to the child feeling even worse. The way that I overcome this problem is to say that the students don't have to contribute if they don't want to, or if they can't. They can simply say the word 'pass' and take a turn when they feel ready.
- *Use a 'conch':* A 'conch', which is explained in more detail further on in this chapter, is basically an item that the students

67

hold when they are taking their turn to speak. There will be times when you are working in a circle that you don't expect everyone to answer around the class. In these cases the conch can be passed to whoever wishes to volunteer.

- *Go both ways:* It is very tempting to always work clockwise around the circle, simply because this is what most of us would naturally do. Sometimes it can be very useful to reverse the direction. This will help to ensure that those at the 'end' of the circle are listening to your instructions, rather than sitting back and waiting to see what the rest of the children do. It will also allow those students at the 'end' a chance to go first.

- *Start in the middle:* Similarly, why not ask a child in the centre of the circle to start the exercise? Again, this helps keep the children on their toes and ensures that everyone gets a chance to start an activity.

- *Watch out for groupings:* I often find when using a circle that small groups of friends stand close to each other. This is no problem if your class are well behaved, but if you have a bunch of troublemakers standing together this can lead to discipline problems. Do watch the way that your class groups itself, and identify any potential problems quickly. Rather than the teacher having to form the circle to avoid behaviour issues, one very quick way of overcoming this problem is to use the 'fruit salad' game. To explain briefly how this works, the teacher gives the names of three or four different fruits (in a tropical fruit salad these might be mango, banana, pineapple and kiwi). The children then call out these names around the circle, so that each child has a fruit name. When the teacher calls out 'banana', all the bananas must swap places, and so on with the different fruits. If the teacher shouts 'fruit salad', everyone must swap around.

There is a huge range of ways in which you can use the structure of a circle to help you teach and practise thinking skills. As you become more accustomed to working with this format you'll hopefully find lots of unusual or original ideas of your own. Here are a few thoughts to help you start.

- *Question and answer:* The teacher poses a question, and then invites answers from the children. The question should preferably be open, rather than closed, and one to which there is no right or wrong answer. To give just one example, you might ask the class: *'What do you think about school uniform, and why?'* The answers here might range from *'I hate it because it's uncomfortable'* to *'It helps keep a sense of discipline in our school.'*
- *Answer and question:* To make things a bit more interesting, why not start by posing an answer, and inviting the children to come up with a range of possible questions. For instance, you could say: *'The answer is yellow, what is the question?'* The children's answers might range from *'What colour are bananas?'* to *'What's my favourite colour?'*
- *Free associations:* You'll find a whole section devoted to free association above. Free association lends itself very well to the structure of a circle. When starting a new topic you might say a single word, and then ask the children to free associate around the circle. The word *'monster'* might lead to a whole host of different thoughts, such as *'scared'*, *'green and scaly'* and *'munch'*.
- *Evaluations:* Circles provide an excellent format for evaluating work, particularly when the class has watched a group presentation and is commenting on how it went. In my experience, children do have a tendency to focus on the negative, so I ask that everyone in the circle says one good thing about what they have seen.

Listing

There's something rather fun about making lists and they have a whole range of potential uses, both inside and outside the classroom. A list might be for a practical purpose, such as the shopping list or the ubiquitous 'Things to do'. (I do wonder whether all teachers are as good at making this type of list as me and as bad at actually getting round to 'doing' the things on their lists?) Alternatively, lists can be used for a more creative purpose, as in the 'Things to put into it' list described below. There is something very satisfying about making a list of jobs and then crossing off items as they are completed. The human brain seems to love the sense of order created by making a list and the sense of conclusion involved when the list is 'done'. A list is also very useful in helping us remember things, whether it is a list of points to make in an examination essay or simply a list of items that we need to buy at the supermarket.

How, then, might we put lists and listing into practice as a structure for thinking? Below I've taken just one idea that will give you an interesting starting point for making use of lists in your own classroom. The lists given involve thinking about a plastic bottle – an easily found item for the teacher to bring in, an object that lends itself to a whole range of uses, and also one that it is good to recycle. When you are asking your children to make lists, you might give them a specific number of items, or you could ask them to find as many points as possible to put on their lists. Here are some ideas for lists connected to your plastic bottle. As you can see, the thinking involved has the potential to take us right across the curriculum.

- List 10 things that you could put inside the bottle. These might be put inside for a purpose (for example, water, to drink), or they could be more creative (for instance, a tiny fairy, to stop her flying away).
- Make a list of as many uses as you can find for the bottle. Again, the list could include the relatively normal, such as 'drink from it'. Hopefully, though, the children would start to think 'outside the box', and come up with some more bizarre and original suggestions.
- List five ways in which the bottle could be used in a scientific experiment. This might include ideas as simple as 'holding water to pour on our plants', or as complex as building some type of still.
- Make a list of different ways that the bottle could be used to make some type of transport. An example might be cutting the base of the bottle off and attaching a balloon to make a mini hot air balloon.

When you've finished writing your lists, you can develop the structure further by taking some of the ideas and running with

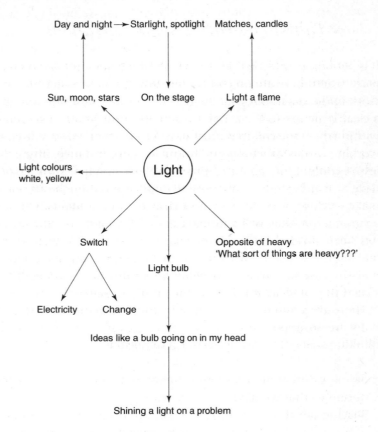

Scared of the dark ⟶ Monsters – *Where the Wild Things Are*

Day and night ⟶ Starlight, spotlight   Matches, candles

Sun, moon, stars   On the stage   Light a flame

Light colours ⟵ **Light**
white, yellow

Switch

Electricity   Change

Light bulb

Opposite of heavy
'What sort of things are heavy???'

Ideas like a bulb going on in my head

Shining a light on a problem

Figure 4.1 Free association

them. So it could be that you get your children performing one of their science experiments, writing a story about the trapped fairy, and so on.

Figure 4.1 shows one possible outcome for a free association on the word 'light'. As you will see from the ideas included, this process is rather different to the traditional brainstorm, as the student is encouraged to take the thoughts where they lead, rather than sticking carefully to the original word. Look too at the way I've structured the diagram, connecting up related areas with the use of arrows.

Thinking: structures and restrictions

It is perhaps surprising that the best thinking does not always take place when there are no constraints. When you're using thinking work in the classroom, you do need to consider how you can give a clear structure to the activities, and also how you can set limits within which the children must stay. As a teacher, you are used to working within structures and restrictions, for instance, fitting the lesson content into a limited time, and ensuring that your lessons have a clear beginning, middle and end. Often, though, we fail to make our use of these structures clear for our students, perhaps assuming that they will automatically understand how the lesson has been divided into different parts. It is actually well worth making the structure of your lessons explicit to your children, so that they start to understand how important (and complex) the structuring of ideas within a set time limit actually is.

There are a number of reasons why these structures and restrictions are so important when it comes to using and developing thinking skills. Here are some of these reasons.

- Using or creating a structure helps us to make sense of the thoughts that we have.
- Placing our thoughts into some kind of order helps encourage the brain to look for and find patterns within the thinking.
- Finding a way to categorize our ideas makes us consider which ideas can be fitted or placed together.
- Using time restrictions gives a strong focus and energy to the thinking.
- Giving word or idea limits forces us to consider what is most important or interesting.

You might use structures and restrictions in a number of different ways. For instance, you could be structuring the way that your children approach the actual tasks, or you might be giving a restricted time limit within which they must work. Below are two ideas for different types of structures or limits that you might like to use in your lessons. These ideas could be adapted to work across the curriculum.

- *Mini stories:* In this exercise, the children are given a slip of paper that contains four words. These words give them a character, a place, an emotion and an object, for instance 'king – forest – angry – stick'. The students are asked to write a 'mini story' using these words, within the time limit of two minutes. One more restriction is added: the story must be *exactly* 20 words long – no more and no less. This idea could easily be altered to work for other subjects, for instance, explaining a historical event or a scientific theory in a limited number of words.
- *2-3-4:* The 2-3-4 activity gives the students two minutes to tell three people four different thoughts or ideas. These ideas might be 'Four things we did in the last lesson', or they could be 'Your four favourite things to eat'. Again, this game could easily be changed to work right across the curriculum. You might also like to adapt the '2-3-4' into '1-2-3' or '4-5-6'.

Sequencing thoughts

Learning how to sequence is probably one of the earliest thinking skills that children develop. When we read fiction to very young children, they begin to see how there is a logical sequence of events within a story. Learning how to sequence a series of thoughts in the correct or most logical order is an important part of understanding how to structure our thinking. This applies not only to stories, but also to work right across the curriculum. For instance, in a cookery lesson the students must understand how to follow recipe instructions in the correct order, otherwise their cooking could be a disaster. Similarly, in a science lesson, the steps of an experiment must be performed in the appropriate sequence if it is going to work.

Sequencing also plays a role in an understanding of cause and effect. For every action within a sequence, there will be a reaction that might move off in a number of different directions. Here are some suggestions for exercises that will help you to develop your students' ability to think about sequencing in a range of different subjects.

- *Sequencing stories:* Write or type out a story on a piece of paper, one sentence on each line, then cut this up into individual sentences. Give each child or group of children the sentences, and ask them to put the story back together in the most logical order. Some interesting discussions could follow on from this, particularly if the story lends itself to a number of potential sequences.
- *Sequencing historical events:* Draw up a timeline (this could be on a wide scale, for instance 2000 BC–2000 AD, or for a much narrower period of history). Working individually or in groups, ask the children to stick a number of historical events onto their timelines. You could develop this exercise by discussing the thinking processes that took place to put each event in the correct order.
- *Sequencing sums:* Give the class a series of different calculations to do, using plus, minus, divide and multiply. Ask them to put these calculations into a rising numerical sequence, using an estimate of what they think the answers will be. They should put the calculation that they believe has the lowest total first, moving up to the highest total last, but without actually working out the answers. This will require them to think carefully about the way that numbers work.
- *Sequencing status:* I use this exercise in drama lessons, and it offers a fun game to get your class thinking about status. Give each child a playing card, using all the cards from 1 (Ace) to King. Explain to them that in this game, the 1 denotes the lowest status, while the King is right at the top of the tree. The children must not look at the card you have given them. Now get the children to hold their cards against their foreheads, making sure that they do not see the number they have been given. The children must now walk around the room, interacting with each other as befits the status of the card on their heads. So it would be that if a child met a 'King', he or she would bow down and grovel, while

if he or she met a '3', this person would be treated with disre-spect. At the end of the game, ask your children to place them-selves in a line in order of status. They must work out the number that they have on their foreheads by judging the way that the others reacted to them.

- *Sequencing word order:* This exercise requires your students to think about the exact meaning of the vocabulary they use. The teacher gives them a series of related words, and they must put these words into the correct order or sequence, jus-tifying the decisions they have made. The order might be to do with size or scale, for instance, from smallest to biggest, or from a weaker emotion to a stronger one. This exercise gets the children thinking about the nuances contained within language, and the importance of accurate expression. You might start the class off with a fairly easy example, for instance, putting different types of buildings into size order. Your example could be: 'house, shed, flat, tower block, castle, mansion'. My chosen order for these words would be: shed, flat, house, mansion, tower block, then castle. Your children might feel that a tower block is bigger than a castle, and you could spend some time discussing which order is more likely to be accurate. Below are some more examples for you to use. You can find lots more synonyms in a thesaurus, and you might even decide to ask the children to make up their own word order puzzles.
  o minuscule, tiny, small, petite, miniature, little;
  o sad, unhappy, upset, miserable, down, gloomy;
  o happy, delighted, overjoyed, ecstatic, joyful, glad.

Structuring discussions

Much of the time our first approach in teaching thinking skills will be via speaking and listening activities. Although we may well be working on written tasks, we are likely to be spending at least some of every lesson that we teach undertaking a discussion about how best to complete these activities. Understanding how to structure discussions is therefore a vital part of learning how to develop our children's thought processes. I have focused the discussion below on the classroom management issues that are involved when using speaking and listening exercises. This includes looking at: how to go about organizing discussion tasks; how we can develop our children's speaking and listening skills; ways of teaching our students how to take notes from spoken presentations, and so on. Hopefully, the tips and advice I give will help you feel more confident about using discussion effectively in your own classroom.

Developing discussion skills

Talking is one of the best structures to use when we want to develop our children's thinking. It gives us the opportunity to 'think out loud', perhaps experimenting with thoughts that are not yet fully formed, and hearing what other people have to say about our ideas. However, it's not as simple as just putting our children into groups, setting them a question to discuss, and then letting them get on with it. Problems will inevitably crop up – the noise levels might rise uncontrollably, the children might drift off task and so on. It's vital therefore that you consider how to structure discussion work within the classroom, and also that you give the class information about how best to undertake the activities concerned. You'll find some ideas about how to do this below. You'll also find some more tips about speaking skills further on in this section (see 'Learning to speak').

- *Tell them how to structure it:* When you set a discussion task, talk with the class about exactly how you wish it to be structured. For instance, in a group activity do you want each person to give one different thought in turn around the circle, before they develop any of the ideas? Alternatively, do you want the group to choose one single idea for more extensive development?
- *Keep them focused:* One of the most difficult issues for the teacher when dealing with group discussion work is that it is almost impossible to ensure that all your children are staying focused and on task at all times. You have no way of listening in on every single group at once, and so you must find other ways of

keeping the children on track. Ideas for achieving this could include:
- o setting a short time limit before you ask for feedback;
- o nominating one member of the group to be 'on task' monitor;
- o ensuring that the task you set is sufficiently engaging to focus the children.

- *Watch the noise levels:* I was once asked in an interview whether I feel that a quiet classroom is a productive classroom. I suspect that this question came about because of my emphasis on the importance of quiet and calm in my book *Getting the Buggers to Behave*. I can appreciate that a certain level of noise is necessary (and indeed vital) for good discussion work. However, I do believe strongly that excessive noise levels simply confuse the students and mean that they find it almost impossible to work. It is practically inevitable that noise levels will go up and up when your children are working in groups: as one group talks louder, so the others have to follow suit to be able to hear. This means that the teacher must take control of the situation. When using group discussions, keep your ears open to assess whether the noise has reached unacceptable levels. At this stage, it is tempting to intervene either by shouting over the children (never a good idea!) or by stopping the class so that you can lecture them. I would avoid both these strategies. Instead, the approach that I would take is to draw a 'noise-o-meter' on the board, and point this out to the children before the discussion begins. When (and if) the noise levels do rise to an unacceptable level, I would simply draw a raised line on the noise-o-meter and point to the board until the class notices.

Learning to listen

Listening is actually a surprisingly complex skill, and one in which we perhaps fail to train our children properly. Being able to listen allows us to take on board the thoughts and ideas of others. It also helps us put a better structure on our own ideas. Here are some tips for teaching your children to become better listeners.

- *Encourage them to make notes:* Speaking is invisible, so it is hard for the listener to catch hold of and retain the ideas that he or she hears. Teach your students how to make notes while someone else is talking. Depending on the age group you teach, you might ask your class to take written notes, or you could use the visual record idea given below.

- *Write down key points:* There is no need for the listener to write down everything that the speaker says. The secret is for the children to learn how to listen out for the key points. These might be single words that summarize a section of what is being said; alternatively, they might be what the children see as the most important parts of the discussion. Do not be surprised if it takes your class quite a while to master this skill – the ability to pick out key ideas is much harder than it might appear. Encourage your students to listen out for the words that actually contain the meaning.

- *Make a visual record:* For younger children who do not yet have the literacy skills required, a visual record will be of as much value as written notes. For instance, the young student might use symbols to stand for different ideas, or quick doodles or diagrams that could act as a reminder about what was said.

- *Use listening exercises:* In the section on focus exercises you will find a couple of examples of listening exercises that you might like to use in your classroom. It is important to train your children in the skill of listening, and to make it a regular part of the work that you do. For instance, you might start each lesson with a short period of listening work, or alternatively use this to finish off your classes. Taking the time to encourage your students to listen is actually very useful in terms of classroom management. You should find that after the children have been doing a listening exercise they are in a calm frame of mind, ready to take a considered approach to the work you set.

- *Make them listen to you:* Becoming a good listener is all about training yourself in how to listen. You can help this process by insisting that the class listens attentively when you are talking, making this a clear and certain expectation of the children's behaviour.

- *Make them focus on you:* It is not enough for the class simply to be silent. You need to ensure that they are all focused fully on you, preferably making eye contact and (hopefully) soaking up your words of wisdom. You'll be able to tell by how they work whether or not they really have been listening to your instructions. Another tip is that if you talk quietly you will encourage the students to listen – they'll have to if they're going to hear you!
- *Make them listen to each other:* As well as ensuring that your students listen with full attention to the teacher, you should also insist on full attention when other children are talking to the class. Again, I would recommend that you have this as a clear and completely unequivocal expectation. My approach has always been that, if somebody does talk when a classmate is presenting his or her ideas, then the presenter must stop and start again. I am totally insistent about this – if it means we work through break, then so be it. (In fact my total and unrelenting insistence means that this rarely happens – after the first couple of times that they have been sanctioned, the class fits in with what I require.)
- *Teach the class to support and acknowledge speakers:* Asking your children to listen very carefully to each other is just one way in which the class can be supportive of each other's spoken work. At the end of an individual or group presentation to the class, I would always insist that my class acknowledges the speaker and gives him or her a reward for the work. This can, of course, be done by the use of applause. However, I dislike the weak, enforced clapping that you tend to get when you ask the class to applaud. Instead, make clapping an important and fun part of the whole speaking and listening process. Practise 'wild' applause with your children, getting them to cheer, whistle and clap as loudly as they can. It's also great fun to practise doing short bursts of extravagant applause by holding up your hand to make a 'cut' signal and seeing how quickly the class can stop.

Learning to speak

I looked above at how you can help your children in using structured discussions to develop their thinking skills. In addition to encouraging them in this skill, it is also important to teach them about how to speak well on an individual basis. This speaking might take place in front of the whole class or it could be within a smaller group setting. Here are some tips about how you can help your students to learn to speak well.

- *Developing confidence:* Some of your children will inevitably be more confident than others when it comes to speaking out in class. It might be that certain children are simply very shy individuals, who do not like or feel comfortable with speaking in front of a large crowd. It could be that their ability with spoken English is as yet quite weak, perhaps because it is not their first language. There are various ways in which you can help to develop the confidence of all the children in your class.
  o *Don't rush it:* Confidence takes time to develop, and trying to push or rush the process will normally have the opposite effect, making the shy individual even more embarrassed to speak out. I would strongly recommend that you don't put less confident individuals on the spot, forcing them to give answers or to make spoken presentations to the whole class before they are ready.
  o *Build up slowly:* Instead, build up the confidence of the shy students gradually by setting activities where they feel less threatened and more supported. For instance, give them the chance to speak within a small group setting, perhaps where they are working with their friends.
  o *Use lavish praise:* If one of your shy children does make a verbal contribution in class, perhaps giving a tentative answer to a question, do ensure that you praise them for this. It could be that praise in front of the class will work well with the individual, or it might be better to make a note of his or her contribution in private: you will need to use your own judgement to decide.
  o *Use confidence building exercises:* There are many speaking exercises that you can use to build up the confidence of your shy speakers gradually. For instance, you can get them working in a setting where the whole class is speaking as a group, and where there is less sense of threat than with an individual

presentation to the class. To give just one example, you might use the 'circle story' exercise explained earlier in this chapter. At first, your quiet children may lack the confidence even to contribute a single word or sentence, so I would recommend that you allow them to say 'pass' if they wish.

- *Speaking properly:* As well as being confident about spoken contributions, you will also want your children to learn how to speak 'properly'. You can help them learn how to do this by explaining exactly what is required and, of course, by showing them an appropriate role model through the way that you address the class. You might like to demonstrate to the class the difference between a 'good' and 'bad' approach to spoken tasks. This could be followed up by some discussion work on the positives or negatives of each approach. The type of skills to look at would include:
  o speaking clearly, so that everyone can understand;
  o talking at a good pace – neither too slow (which could be boring) nor too fast (which might make them unintelligible);
  o speaking at a volume which allows everyone to hear, including those sitting at the back of the room;
  o using the appropriate tone of voice for the content of what is being said, for instance, giving expression to a story;
  o displaying confident body language that encourages the audience to watch and believe in the speaker;
  o keeping the audience's attention by making the content interesting and engaging;
  o making eye contact with members of the audience, and ensuring that they are listening at all times;
  o dealing with any interruptions in an appropriate manner, for instance, pausing if someone talks over you.
- *Vocal warm-ups:* If your children are working on spoken thinking activities, it is a good idea to use a quick vocal warm-up to energize and engage them. Many of these vocal warm-ups will also have the additional benefits of using different thinking processes. To give just one example, you might use a game of word tennis at the start of a lesson. Get your children to stand in pairs, opposite a partner. When you say 'go', they must quickly say one word each in turn, as though playing tennis but

with vocabulary as the ball. The words must be associated in some way (for instance opposites, or just free associations or connections that the children make in their minds). The idea is to keep talking at all times: a child who pauses loses one life. You could start them off with five lives each, and see which pair can keep going the longest.

- *Structuring ideas:* When we're speaking our thoughts out loud, it is important that we find a way to structure the ideas that we give. As with many other areas of learning, it really pays to give your children a framework for their speaking. Make the way that you wish their ideas to be structured as explicit as possible. For instance, you might ask the children to use a particular sentence structure, such as *'I think x, because x'*. This will help them to justify the statements that they make, a vital step in developing and sustaining logical arguments.

- *Something to talk about:* I feel very strongly that we need to engage our children fully in their learning, that we should make the topic or process as interesting and appealing as possible. When you are asking your children to make verbal contributions in class, it helps a lot if the subject of the discussion is one that really holds their attention, or if the format you are using is very attractive to them. For instance, you might use the chat show idea given in Chapter 3 to give them an engaging format within which to think.

Taking turns

As I noted above, it is inevitable that some children will be more confident than others when it comes to speaking and listening tasks, and consequently may dominate group or class discussions. The teacher must therefore take care that he or she structures the work so that the students learn how to take turns. There are a whole variety of ways in which this can be done. Here are a few ideas for you to use in your own classroom.

- *Circle time:* This approach is very popular in primary schools, although it is much less well used in the secondary sector (perhaps because of the difficulty of controlling large numbers of older children, who have a tendency to drift off task when asked to listen to each other). You will find a detailed description of circle time earlier in this chapter. Circle time can be built into each day, perhaps as a way of pulling the class together in the morning, and its regular use will give the teacher an excellent structure for developing thinking. Circle time has a great number of benefits: not least, that it gives the class a sense of working together as a group, in what might be called a 'community of enquiry'.

− *The 'conch':* In William Golding's novel *The Lord of the Flies*, a group of boys are stranded on a desert island. At the start of the book they try to set up a society, one based on the democratic principles that they are aware of from their lives back home. As part of this process they use a conch shell as a way of calling meetings, and of denoting whose turn it is to speak during the discussions. You can use this idea in your own classroom to encourage your children to take turns. You do not necessarily have to use a conch − a 'speaking stick' or other item will have just the same impact. It's important to make sure that the object you use has good visual appeal, so that the children actually want to get a chance to hold it (and consequently to speak to the class). It is also a good idea to introduce it in a rather reverential fashion, making it appear magical and of great import.

− *Keep a record:* It's hard for teachers to keep an eye on the class as a whole, and to ensure that everyone has a chance to contribute their thoughts and ideas, or to give answers to the questions that we pose. We perhaps tend to assume that we will automatically know whether our children are making an equal amount of verbal contributions to the class, but in my own experience this is not necessarily the case. One way to ensure that you get all the students contributing in a fairly equal manner is to keep a written record. Obtain a list of your children's names, and then place a tick beside the name of the student as he or she answers a question or gives a thought during whole class thinking tasks. When you do this you will probably start to notice a pattern in which some children contribute frequently whereas others sit quietly and hardly offer their ideas at all.

- *Encourage the reticent contributor:* If you do notice that some students are less confident about making contributions then try to encourage these individuals to become more vocal. It is up to you how you do this, and you will need to use your professional judgement to decide which approaches are appropriate. For instance, you might direct a question at a specific child, particularly those who do not normally contribute. Be careful when you do this, however, not to put these children 'on the spot' and make them even less confident about offering their ideas.
- *Everyone has an answer:* Another idea is to ensure that every student in the class has a potential answer to give when you do ask a question. In order to do this, after you've posed your question tell the class that you want everyone to come up with an answer, even though not everyone's answer will be heard. Give the children some 'thinking time', perhaps two or three minutes, before hearing one or more answers to your question.
- *In groups:* When our children are working in groups, the tendency can be for the naturally confident ones to take over, and for the quieter children to allow this to happen. There are a number of different approaches that you can use to help you avoid this. For example, you might:
  o nominate a group leader to lead the discussion, ensuring that this is not a normally dominant child;
  o set up a version of 'circle time' or 'the conch' within the groups, whereby each child is required to contribute in turn;
  o ensure that the groups are formatted so that the quieter individuals work together, and the more dominant personalities are placed within the same group.

Working with groups

The group offers an excellent format or structure within which to develop your children's thinking. As a drama teacher, group work is the backbone of much of the teaching that I do. Of course, there is a place for soliloquies and individual presentations in the drama class. However, the majority of the improvisations, performances and other activities that I set will be done in pairs or in larger groups. On occasions, I will even ask the whole class to work together as a single group – a very interesting exercise in group dynamics and in teacher (and student) control! Group work provides us with a wonderful way of developing a number of important skills with our students. For a start they must co-operate with each other if the work is going to be successful. You'll find some more skill areas that group work develops listed below (see 'Learning vital skills').

Group work plays a crucial role in the development of thinking skills. For a start, it is only within a group (whether of two children or a whole class) that discussion can take place. As we have established above, speaking and listening activities offer an extremely constructive format for many areas of thinking. Here are some ideas about why group work is so important and useful within the classroom.

- *Sharing and exchanging ideas:* Although thinking is, on the whole, an individual process, learning to share and exchange ideas with peers will help our children to work with their own thoughts. As the children bounce their ideas around within the group, these thoughts are quickly changed, developed or extended.
- *Feedback:* The process of feedback that takes place within the group setting will help our children to clarify their thoughts, to see what is positive about an idea, and so on. Your students might also be offering different opinions on a similar issue, and this will show them how different viewpoints can be equally as valid as their own.
- *Development of ideas:* The process of batting ideas around a group helps with the development of these ideas. The group might take one idea as a starting point and then add lots of people's thoughts together to see where this leads them.
- *Learning vital skills:* Working in a group allows our children to develop some of the most vital learning skills. They must concentrate carefully when others are talking, so that they can

hear and understand what is being said. They must also co-operate with the rest of the group. In addition, they must learn how to take into consideration what other people have to say, and to be supportive of their fellow group members.

Creating groups

Because so many thinking activities require the use of group work, it is important that we think carefully about how we are actually going to put our students together. You might feel that organizing groups is a fairly straightforward task, but in fact the way that we set up the groups will have a strong impact on how successfully the thinking exercises work. I do believe that it's important for the teacher to actually make a conscious decision about whether friendship groupings will work best in his or her classroom, rather than simply using them because they are easiest to organize. It is, of course, possible for the teacher to use a mixture of different systems, seeing how each one works over a period of time. The various advantages and disadvantages of using different systems of groupings are discussed below.

- *Friendship groupings:* It can be very tempting to allow our students to choose their own groups when we want them to work together. The comments below about the advantages and disadvantages of this system will help you decide whether it is the best approach for you and your class.
  o *Advantages:* The students do tend to work well together when they are with their friends and this lessens the likelihood of quarrels and disagreements arising. In addition, this system is probably the easiest for the teacher to organize. We can simply say *'Get yourself into groups'* and then move straight on with the task at hand.
  o *Disadvantages:* On the downside, the use of friendship groupings can mean that those children who are less popular do tend to get left out. The result of this is that the teacher has to allocate these students to groups, and this can cause resentments that can lead in turn to tensions arising. In addition,

you may well find that when they are working with their friends your students tend to go off task more readily. The temptation is to talk socially rather than to focus on the tasks. Finally, when you allow the children to decide on their own groups, you will often find that the boys and girls divide themselves along gender lines.

- *Teacher-chosen groupings:* As an alternative to letting the students choose their own groups, the teacher might decide to form the groupings for his or herself. Again, this approach has both its plus and minus points.
  o *Advantages:* With this system the teacher has control of who works with whom. In a class where behaviour is an issue this method of grouping allows the teacher to keep the poorly behaved children apart. If the groups are well arranged, the children will find it easier to stay on task. Using teacher-chosen groupings also allows you to carefully integrate those children who might normally be left out of the work. This could mean putting quiet children together, so that they don't become overshadowed. It might also mean ensuring that the child who has few if any friends does not get left out when the class is picking the groupings. You will also be able to achieve a good mixture of male and female students within each group.
  o *Disadvantages:* This approach does require quite a lot of pre-organization from the teacher. You will need to work out the groups carefully beforehand. If this is not done with sufficient thought, there is the possibility that you might end up with groups where difficult personalities are having to work together, and this can lead to conflicts.
- *Random groupings:* My preference is often to use random groupings, particularly when the group work is only going to take place for a short space of time. There are a whole range of ways in which to organize random groups, but perhaps the easiest is via a numbering system. Here's how to do it: count how many children there are in the class, then divide this by the number of students you want in each group. The children then count out loud up to this number around the room, giving them each a number that denotes their group. So, if the teacher wants to

have groups of three in a class of 27, the children would need to count around the class or circle up to nine. The number 1s would then work together, the number 2s, and so on. Here are some thoughts about the potential pluses and minuses of this system.

o *Advantages:* Organizing random groupings is a very straight-forward method by which to work. There can be no argument between the students about who works together. The system is not controlled by the teacher but just works in the way that chance sets it up. You should end up with a good mixture of male and female within each group.

o *Disadvantages:* Unfortunately, the random nature of this system means that you may also end up with some dodgy groupings by accident. In addition, the children quickly suss out the numbering method described above, and put themselves into a certain order so that they end up working with their friends. (Mind you, this very action demonstrates a pretty impressive display of thinking!) To overcome this, simply start the counting from a different point in the class, for instance, in the middle of the circle.

Structuring complex thinking

When it comes to the later years of the secondary school, your students will be starting to work with complex thought patterns and processes. For instance, you could be asking them to write an essay that involves examining a topic in detail. It is at this stage that you will need to teach your class about how to structure complex thinking. In order to give you some tips on how to go about this, I would like to use the example of the way in which I write my books. When I do this, I use a process that allows my early thinking to develop over the course of time. It is only gradually that I enlarge these initial thoughts into the detailed ideas and complex structures that go together to make up a whole book. In *Getting the Buggers to Write*, I use the metaphor of creating a building to help describe this process. When you're aiming to develop the structuring of complex thinking with your students, using outlines in a similar way can provide a very valuable way of getting from the initial 'first ideas' to the fully developed 'finished product'.

You'll find a plan below that describes the process in more detail. As you'll see, the different areas are divided into 'brainstorming' (gathering initial information), 'structuring' (putting the ideas in some sort of appropriate order), 'developing' (expanding the ideas into more complex thoughts) and 'finishing off' (tidying up the whole shebang). Of course, this is not necessarily a chronological process. Sometimes the areas overlap, and sometimes I find myself going backwards to reorder my ideas where necessary. These exact same processes can be used in your own classroom when you're working on the more complex thinking structures. Below the description of the process with which I develop my books you'll find a similar list in italics that shows you how this structure might be applied to the writing of an essay.

Brainstorming

(Book)

- Finding the initial idea for a book and agreeing it with my editor.
- Choosing a title for the book. (I find this a useful source of inspiration for my writing, particularly when it comes to considering style, although it could in theory come at any point during the project.)
- Making an initial list of the chapter headings.
- Doing any research or fact finding that is required.

(Essay)

- *Finding the initial idea or focus for an essay, and checking this with the teacher.*
- *Deciding on a suitable question for the essay to answer.*
- *Writing an initial plan of what might be included in each paragraph.*
- *Gathering together the relevant information, for instance, facts, quotations, and so forth.*

Structuring

- Exploring a logical order for the chapters.
- Listing ideas for the different headings that could come within each chapter.
- Putting these headings into an appropriate sequence.

- *Looking at a logical order for the paragraphs within the essay.*
- *Making a more detailed list or plan of what will be explored within each paragraph.*
- *Ensuring that these ideas are arranged in the appropriate sequence.*

Developing

- Developing the ideas and writing the content that goes within the section headings of each chapter.
- Moving sections around to see which order works best.
- Lateral thinking about the ideas that I've already included, and where these might lead. (This often takes me off in another direction, and can require the re-ordering of the material that I've already included.)
- Re-reading each chapter after it is finished, and editing the ideas and writing as necessary. This could be to do with writing style, or it might be about the actual content of the book.
- Cutting any excess or irrelevant material, or anything that I feel doesn't work properly.

- *Development of ideas and writing of each paragraph in turn.*
- *Re-ordering the paragraphs as necessary, to create a logical and sustained argument.*
- *Exploring any lateral connections that occur during the writing process, and again re-ordering the paragraphs as required.*
- *Re-reading each paragraph on completion, and making any editing changes that might improve it. As with the book, this edit could be about adaptations to style, or to content.*
- *Cutting any material that does not need to be included (for instance, to stick to a specific word count).*

Finishing off

- Setting the text aside for a while (a few days if possible) and then re-reading it from a distance. Although it's hard to read your own writing dispassionately, having a little time away from the manuscript is a great help.
- Making any small (or sometimes large) changes to the content that seem necessary after this read through.
- Checking the entire book through for errors of spelling, punctuation and grammar, as well as for any factual mistakes.
- Presenting the finished book in the appropriate format (for a manuscript this means double-spaced, and with a specific layout).

- *If possible, leaving at least a day before making an objective re-read of the essay.*
- *Making minor (or sometimes major) alterations as required after this re-reading.*
- *Checking for accuracy – whether this is about the way that it is written or the content that has been included.*
- *Handing in the completed essay in the correct format, for instance, word processing it and leaving margins for the teacher's comments.*

5

Memory

This chapter deals with memory, and gives you a brief introduction to this particular thinking skill. Typically, we do tend to class ourselves as having either a 'good' or a 'bad' memory. Perhaps we don't really believe that it is possible for us to improve our memories. However, as with any other area of learning, there are many ways in which we can develop and increase our power in this particular area of thinking. Some of the techniques that I describe below may strike you as bizarre and far too weird to actually work. However, this is a big part of their secret. When we make very strange and imaginative links our brains are far more likely to retain the information that we are seeking to memorize.

If you're interested in studying the fascinating subject that is memory, then you can find some really excellent books on the market that will help you explore this area further. I would highly recommend those written by Tony Buzan, an expert on the whole area of using the brain. In particular, *Use your Memory* (BBC Books) goes into a great deal of detail on the subject.

When you're working on developing your students' memories, it pays to be really explicit with them about how this can be done. It is not enough simply to expect them to work out how to remember things by themselves – you need to give your class the tools by which this is made possible. You might be helping your children to learn and remember their spellings or advising them about how to revise and remember facts for an examination. By teaching them some of the techniques and tricks described in this chapter you will unlock the fantastic potential that we all have for increasing and improving our memories. I cover a range of ideas here, including how memory works, how to make things more memorable, a quick guide to memory systems, ways of remembering spellings, and the use of memory for revision.

Memory: an overview

Learning how to memorize things, and to do it well, is crucial for our students. Being able to remember facts, figures and other important information allows us to function effectively. Memory plays a huge role in our everyday world – from simple tasks such as remembering the items that we need to buy at the shops, to remembering a friend's birthday, or the time of an important appointment. Within the school environment, memory is particularly vital in a society like ours that puts such emphasis on passing examinations. Regardless of our personal feelings about the value of testing, being able to memorize facts, figures, techniques, and so on will allow our children to do well in their exams.

Although we might feel that some people have a 'good' memory, whereas others do not, it is in fact possible to develop the skill of remembering. A person who appears to have a good memory will probably be either subconsciously or consciously using techniques that are easily learned by others. We can use thinking skills to develop the structures and links that open the door to good memory. We can certainly train ourselves to remember better and in so doing develop our thinking skills and our ability to use our brains.

How do we remember?

If you think back to when you were a child, there will be certain people, events or objects that stick in your memory, remaining vivid long after the time. Exploring why this happens can help give us an insight into exactly how memory works. For example, you might remember the following.

- An event during which you were particularly happy and excited, such as a holiday or a birthday party.
- An object, for instance, a toy, to which you were very closely attached.
- A time when you experienced strong emotions. These might be negative as well as positive, for instance, fear, sadness or anger. (Note: it is worth bearing in mind that the brain does have a tendency to better retain the positive, and to avoid returning to the more negative feelings.)
- A place that had special meanings for you, such as your grandparents' house or a beach that you visited with your parents.
- A person to whom you were strongly attached, for instance, a close childhood friend or a beloved uncle.
- A smell that you either loved or loathed, for instance, the aroma of a particular dish being cooked.

These memories stick in the mind for many reasons, not least because of the powerful associations they create within us. In fact it is quite amazing how vivid images can be seen in the mind's eye, long after the event has passed into history. The same applies to strong emotions, and as children we are subject to the force of extreme feelings far more than when we become adults.

Here's a quick exercise to show you how powerful your own memory is in returning to the past to conjure up a world that you might have thought long forgotten. This exercise has slight similarities to the process by which people are hypnotized so that they recollect events from their past.

- Choose one moment from your childhood that still remains strong in your memory. This might be an event, a place, an object, a person, and so on.
- Close your eyes for a moment and take yourself back to this time. Spend a few minutes recreating the memory in your mind's eye.
- Look around yourself and move about within the picture that you have created.
- Use all your senses – what can you see, hear, touch, taste and smell at this moment?

- Tap into your emotional side – how did you feel at this specific time? Were you happy, sad, excited, angry?
- Can you remember anything that was said? Try to bring back the sound of the people, the way they were talking, the emotions they were feeling.

The power of stories

If you think for a moment about all the books that you've read, you will see that certain stories stick in your memory. I'm an avid reader of books, sometimes devouring one or two per week, but there are only a few that I can strongly recollect. Consider why these particular stories have stayed in your mind. It could be that the author portrayed an especially strong character, perhaps one with whom you identified. It might be that the events in the story had some relevance to your own life. Or it could simply be that the writer created such a powerful setting or engrossing storyline that it stuck with you permanently. Our minds have an incredible ability that allows us to imagine a story fully, conjuring up images, places, scents, objects, and so on. The power of our imagination seems to brand some of these pictures into the memory so that they are retained without much effort at all.

We can use the power of stories to help our children use and develop their memories. For instance, if you wanted your class to memorize a list of items, facts or points, you could ask the students to make up a story that contains these particular objects or ideas. The story must be as vivid as possible, using big images, powerful actions, detailed descriptions, unusual ideas, all the senses. The example story below shows you how this technique can work. The items that the student wishes to remember are those from a session of Kim's game (see further on in the chapter for an explanation of this game). The items to be memorized are:

- a pen;
- a mirror;
- a ball of string;
- a matchbox;
- a box of tissues.

Here's the story that the child might create:

A princess was sitting looking in her magic mirror. The mirror was huge – it took up the whole of one wall in her bedroom. In the mirror she could see another room, and in this room sat a prince. The prince was writing a letter with a beautiful pen. The pen was made of gold and diamonds, and it glinted in the candlelight. As the princess watched, a single tear fell down the prince's cheek. He reached out and picked up a box of tissues. Just like the pen, the box of tissues was made of gold and diamonds, and the tissues themselves were all the colours of the rainbow. The prince wiped the tear from his face and continued writing.

Later that evening, the princess decided to try to contact the prince through her magic mirror. She took down a huge spell book from her shelf and opened it at the page entitled 'How to contact someone through a magic mirror'. The spell was complicated, involving frogs, spiders, and all sorts of grisly creatures. But the two most important ingredients, without which the spell would not work, were a huge ball of string and a tiny, miniature matchbox. The princess was devastated – many years ago her father had banned balls of string and matchboxes from the kingdom. There was no way that she could complete the spell.

Memory systems

Systems for improving the memory have been with us for a long time. The ancient Greeks developed the first complex ideas about how memory works, and how we might improve our ability to remember. Today, you will find adverts in the newspapers that promise to give you advice that will improve your memory beyond recognition. The quest for memory is one that has fascinated and interested human beings right through the ages.

The term 'mnemonics', with which you will probably be familiar, describes *aides-mémoire*, terms made up to assist us in remembering something. An example is the rhyme 'i before e, except after c', which helps us remember the correct letter order of i and e. You might also know the saying 'Richard of York gave battle in vain', which is designed to assist in remembering the colours of the rainbow.

Our brains work in such a way that in order to remember things we need to make connections. These links or associations take advantage of the way that our memory functions best – we take something that we have already retained, and hook it up to another idea, fact or item. The number system described below is a perfect example of how this works. Numbers are something that pretty much all of us know – we can all count from one to 10. The system uses this fact to allow us to hook additional images and ideas onto these numbers and consequently to retain these in the mind.

Making things memorable

Memory systems require us to make the items we wish to remember more memorable in some way. There is a whole range of approaches that we can take to do this. The key to remembering is to work with the way our brains work, creating powerful images and using our imaginations to the full. It's also important to structure the things that you wish to remember in a way that works best for your own particular memory style. You'll find some more ideas about how to do this in the section at the end of this chapter on memory and revision. The thoughts below will give you a good starting point for making things more memorable.

- *Rhyme and rhythm:* If you try to memorize a passage of prose, then try again with a rhyming poem, you'll see how much more easily the poem sticks in your mind. There are various factors involved here: the rhymes themselves make the poem more memorable and there is also the rhythmic nature of the language within poetry. We can use these factors to help our children remember, by showing them strategies and memory systems that involve rhymes and rhythms.
- *Mnemonic sayings:* As I explained above, a mnemonic is a device that makes something more memorable. As a child I learnt a saying that you will probably know as well: 'Never eat Shredded Wheat'. This mnemonic is designed to help you remember the directions of the compass in the correct order – North East South West. It has stuck with me right through the

years, and in fact I refer back to it in my head right up to this day when I need to work out directions.

- *Links:* Memory systems encourage us to make links between 'hooks' that we find it easy to retain in our memories (for instance numbers, as explained above) and what it is we wish to remember. These hooks succeed because the way that our brains work is all about finding, making and retaining connections. The number system described below shows you one example of how using links can work.

- *The first thing that comes to mind:* Carrying on with the idea of creating connections, if you wish to make a link to aid your memory it is worth going with the first thing that comes to your mind. To explain further, say for example that you were trying to remember the name of a girl called Sally. The first thought that came into your mind on hearing the name might be the phrase 'long tall Sally'. You would then need to use this phrase to create a link between the two. So, if Sally were a tall child you might emphasize a picture of Sally as being really really tall and long in your mind. The next time you saw her, the image of a 'long tall Sally' would hopefully pop into your brain, enabling you to recall her name.

- *Stressing what's hard to remember:* Many years ago, I trained to be a professional dancer. We would have to remember long and complicated series of steps for our performances. It was then that I worked out a technique for retaining those parts of the dances that were particularly troublesome to recall. What I would do is simply focus on the bits that I would most often forget, rather than worrying about retaining the whole dance. By focusing on these steps, the rest would come easily to mind. This technique can be applied to the whole area of learning and can be very helpful to our children in the classroom. For instance, when trying to remember a spelling, encourage the child to put most focus on the part of that word that he or she always gets wrong. Similarly, when aiming to remember a list of factual points, ask your students to pick out the one that they find most difficult to retain and to put a strong emphasis on this particular idea.

- *Vivid images:* In the section that follows, you'll see an explanation of the whole idea of using vivid images. These mind pictures are useful in all areas of memory but particularly so in the type of system described below. The idea is that the more vivid the image that is created in the mind, the better the brain will be able to retain and recall that information.

 — *Repetition:* Perhaps the simplest and most commonly used way of retaining information is through the use of repetition. Many students will use repeated readings as a way of revising in the hope that this will help them remember the information. Hearing a word, name or other detail over and over again does tend to 'stick it' in our minds. For instance, we might use repetition to help us memorize our children's names, as described in the section 'Remembering people'. Children who read a great deal will tend to be good spellers, simply because they have seen the vocabulary repeated so many times. This approach does have its drawbacks in that it can take a great deal of time and a large number of recurrences for the memory to be retained and at the end of the day we may not actually be able to recall the item after all. It is in fact not necessarily the most effective way of approaching this particular thinking task, and other more targeted systems can provide us with a far better basis for our learning.

Number systems

There is a whole range of different systems by which you can help your students to improve their memories. The factor that unites them is the use of hooks or associations to help the mind make the connections that are so vital for retention. You can find many different memory systems explained in Tony Buzan's book *Use your Memory*. Below is a brief outline of one of the most basic and simple systems, which involves the use of numbers to create those vital hooks.

The number system for remembering works on the basis of choosing rhyming words that link numbers to words (usually objects), and then making strong and dramatic links and associations between those things and the items that you wish to recall. As we saw above, the mind finds it particularly easy to recall rhymes (probably partly because there are relatively few words that rhyme together). So, the number-rhyme links are a good way of giving yourself a basis for remembering. By 'hooking' what you want to recall onto your own number associations, you work with the way that your brain remembers, by making connections. Again, you can find a very detailed explanation of this technique in Tony Buzan's book.

First of all, we need to consider the various ways in which we might make these strong, dramatic links between the number words and the items that we want to memorize. Below are some thoughts about how this can be done. You can see some examples of specific associations a little further on in this section.

- *Use of the senses:* When we're aiming to remember, we need to engage fully with the material that we wish to recall. We can do this by using all our senses. As we saw previously in this chapter ('How do we remember?'), the mind recollects highly sensual experiences, often in great detail. So, when you're helping your children to develop their memories, encourage them to bring their senses into play: seeing things vividly, hearing noises, smelling aromas, and so on. The examples below show you how using your senses can help in remembering.
- *Colours:* Similarly, we can encourage our minds to hold onto colours as a way of helping us to remember. The colours that we visualize should be vivid or unusual, to help us in retaining them. So, in the story given in the section on 'The power of stories', the tissues are rainbow coloured. Similarly, the baked beans used in the example below are a vivid orange colour. Colours are closely linked with emotion and feelings, and again we can use this fact to aid our memories. For instance, the colour red tends to be linked to passion and heat. If you were trying to remember a list of things that made a character in a story angry, you might picture these items in your head coloured in a bright red.
- *Size:* The more enormous or minuscule the image that we visualize, the more vividly it will be portrayed and retained in our mind's eye. Again, you can see how this might work in the number associations described below.
- *Action:* Creating a scene in which vivid action takes place will help your brain to recall the scenario. If you think about stories

that you can easily bring to mind (whether in books, on the television or films), you will notice that these often have strong, energetic action scenes portrayed in them.

- *Just plain weird:* The brain seems to retain weird, unusual images more fully than normal ones. The events that stick in your mind do tend to be ones that are out of the ordinary, rather than the type that happen daily. Teach your children to make use of this fact, particularly if using a memory system like the one explained below. Notice how the images that I use in the examples are often strange, bizarre ones, that the mind will more easily recall.

Here is an outline of how the number system for memory works.

- The first step is to create your own number/object hooks. You can choose any word that rhymes with the number in question. It is best to decide on a word that instantly springs into your mind when you look for a rhyme associated with each number. So you might come up with:
  o One – Gun
  o Two – Glue
  o Three – Tree
  o Four – Door
  o Five – Hive
  o Six – Bricks
  o Seven – Heaven
  o Eight – Gate
  o Nine – Line
  o Ten – Pen
- Next, you need to fix the hooks you have chosen in your mind. Do this by closing your eyes and picturing each item in turn. Make the images as vivid as possible, using some of the techniques described above ('Making things memorable'). Repeat this step several times, until you are sure that each word has been fully retained in your memory.
- Now take a list of items, facts or ideas that you wish to remember. This might, for instance, be the key words from your

revision plans (see 'Memory and revision'), or anything else that you want to be able to recall. Your aim is to connect up these words to the hooks you have devised. To take an example that will work for you outside of school (and hopefully show you how useful the system is!), if I was heading to the shops I might want to remember to buy:

o baked beans;
o a loaf of bread;
o butter;
o milk;
o cheese;
o potatoes;
o a birthday card;
o nappies;
o a lottery ticket;
o shampoo.

- To demonstrate how the technique can improve your memory, I'd like you to take a quick test (apologies if you've recently endured SATs or Ofsted). This will help you put yourself in the place of your students, faced with a list of facts, items or ideas to memorize. Have a look at the list above, and give yourself a minute or so to memorize it. Then turn the book over and see how many of the groceries you can recall. Now follow the instructions below to help you memorize the list using the number system.

- Link each item on the list with one of the numbers, by creating a strong image in your imagination, and taking a few moments to visualize each one. To get you started, you might have:

  o One – Gun (baked beans). Picture yourself holding a huge gun and shooting directly at the can of beans. Watch in your mind's eye as the bullet speeds towards the can, and then the beans explode and splatter themselves across the wall, leaving a bright orange stain. (If you don't feel that the gun image is an appropriate one to use with your children, you could replace it with another rhyming word such as 'sun' or 'bun'.)

  o Two – Glue (a loaf of bread). Imagine the tiniest loaf of bread in the world. You go to pick it up, and it sticks to your hand. It is so tiny that you are fearful of pulling it off your hand, in case you damage it. You tug at it gently, but it refuses to budge. You pull again and again, and the bread stretches until it becomes the most enormous loaf in the world.

o Three – Tree (butter). See yourself standing below a tree, staring up at the huge branches, swaying in the wind. At the top of the tree is your ball, which has become stuck. You need to climb up the tree to collect it. You try to pull yourself up to the lowest branch, but the trunk of the tree is covered in butter, and you cannot get a grip. You try again and again, but the butter smears itself all over your hands and there is no way you can reach the ball. You look at your hands and the butter glows bright yellow. The heat of the sun makes it drip to the ground.

– Once you have created a series of images that work for you, try again with the test of memory and compare the results with your previous attempt. You should hopefully find that you can recall every item on the list.

Remembering spellings

In the past, many children were expected to remember their spellings but were never taught how to do this. The weekly spelling test would check which of the students had been able to remember how to spell certain words and those who were unable to do so probably felt like complete failures. Traditional methods of learning spellings, such as repeatedly writing down a word, or simply looking at the vocabulary for a long period of time, might have worked in the short term. However, this type of memorizing is generally very short lived. Without the strategies to retain the learning, and also the ability to apply it to future learning, this rote approach is fairly meaningless.

Happily, many teachers these days are becoming aware that the learning of spelling is in fact closely connected to the use of thinking skills. As a child I was always 'good' at spelling, simply because I was able to work out my own strategies for approaching the

103

memorization of words. We need to pass on these techniques to our students, making them explicit and clear. We also need to show our children how to delve deeply into the words that they encounter, making connections and working with the vocabulary to help make it more memorable. Here are a few different strategies and approaches that you can share with your own students. For more ideas about remembering spellings, see my book *Getting the Buggers to Write*.

- *Connect words and objects:* The more often we see a word, the more likely we are to spell it correctly. The old-fashioned approach of drumming a word into our minds by constant repetition has at least some validity. This is also why those children who read a great deal will tend to be better spellers. They have seen each word so often that their minds perform an almost physical check on whether a word 'looks' right. Consequently, labelling the objects in your classroom is a good way to encourage the retention of certain words. Many primary teachers will do this naturally, to help with literacy skills. However, secondary teachers do tend to overlook this useful technique, which can aid spelling across the curriculum. Depending on the age and needs of your children, you might label subject-specific items, such as test tubes or Bunsen burners in the science lab. Alternatively, you might focus on labelling more general objects, such as the board, the windows and so on.
- *Use visual memory tricks:* As we saw in the previous section, the mind works in such a way that visual images are more easily retained and recalled. For this reason, it is very helpful to show your children visual ways in which they can remember words. For instance, a primary teacher working on the word 'bed' could tell their children to make a 'bed' with his or her fingers to spell the word. In this way, the children learn to put the 'b' and 'd' the correct way round.
- *Look at the shape of words:* Ask your children to explore the shape of the words that they are trying to spell. By examining which parts of the words are tall or short, or which come under or over the lines on a page, you will help them in memorizing the visual appearance of a word.

- *Relationships:* If you can find a way to relate the word being learned to another word your students already know, this will give the children those vital 'hooks' on which to hang their memory. For instance, the word 'beautiful' relates to 'beauty', the word 'because' to 'cause'. When you come across a new word, you might get your children to make a list of all the similar words they can find. This will help them start to see how words are related and interconnected.

- *Split words into syllables:* Splitting a word up into its separate sounds will help your students to remember a spelling. For example, splitting 'February' up into 'Feb / ru / ary', or 'particularly' into 'par / tic / u / lar / ly'.

- *Remember the bit you always forget:* As I pointed out earlier, it's a good idea to focus on the things that you find most hard to recall. Looking at the two words in the example above, the mistakes would tend to be missing the 'r's out, because these are the silent sounds. So, when explaining strategies for spelling these words correctly, tell your students to emphasize the difficult part of the word in their heads. They could do this as the word is spelt, rather than said, for instance, by stressing the 'ru' sound in February and the 'lar' sound in particularly.

- *Memory links:* You can find links between the meaning of some words and their spelling, to assist your children in retaining them. To remember the word 'exaggerate', note the fact that it has two 'g's rather than one. This links to the whole idea of exaggerating. Similarly, the word 'too' means very or a lot, and has more than one 'o'.

- *Picture the words:* As I pointed out above, the best readers are often very good at spelling too. They are able to 'see' a word and know instinctively whether it is right or wrong, because they have seen it so many times during the course of reading books. Encourage your students to visualize words in their heads, spelt correctly. Alternatively, if a child always spells the same word wrong, tell him or her to picture the wrong spelling, with a huge red cross through it.

Remembering people

The ability to remember people's names is an incredibly useful skill. Being able to call someone by (the right) name gives a powerful impression, and suggests a strong interest in who they are and what they can do. One of the teachers that I interviewed for my book *The Guerilla Guide to Teaching* gave me a wonderful quote which I feel sums up the power of being able to address our students by name: *'The sweetest sound to any child is the sound of his or her own name.'* Nowhere is this more true than in the classroom, where the teacher who can identify each child by name has an advantage in relating to, and controlling, the class as a whole.

Each year, teachers are faced with the difficult task of remembering large numbers of different students. Depending on your age range and subject, you might need to memorize the names of between 30 and 200 students (or perhaps even more). If you cannot retain and recall these names, you will find yourself experiencing difficulties in all areas of your teaching – from classroom and behaviour management to writing reports and talking to parents. Consequently, using memory techniques to remember people's names is potentially extremely useful to us as teachers, as well as offering us helpful memory strategies and thinking skills to teach our children.

There are a number of approaches that you may find helpful when you are aiming to remember your students' names. The ideas below will help you get started on this task. I also give details of a specific memory system for the retention of names further on in this section.

- *Start right away:* Remembering names is crucial, so it really does pay to get started on the job right at the beginning of your time with a class. You can use games and activities designed to help you remember names as a way of getting to know a class, before you begin delivering the curriculum. Some of the exercises that you might use are described below. Time spent on this task is never wasted time. Being able to say *'Gemma, stop that right now'* or *'Ben, that's a wonderful piece of work'* is so much more powerful with the name included. Your children will enjoy these exercises and it gives them the chance to get to know their classmates as well.

- *Repetition:* A good way to make a start on learning names is to hear or see the names over and over again. When you first introduce yourself to a child, ask for his or her name and repeat it back, asking for clarification about pronunciation if required. Aim to use activities that actually involve working with your children's names. You can find some suggestions below. Many teachers do in fact rely solely on repetition to remember the names of the students that they teach, hoping that over time the names will become embedded in their brains. Eventually this does work to some extent but you can make the process easier and quicker by using some other strategies as well. In addition, the problem with relying solely on repetition is that there are some names that never seem to stick. These are often the names of the quieter students, who hardly ever contribute or cause you difficulties. I know that I have faced this problem myself and it has created issues when it comes to report-writing time. It can also lead to us tending to ignore or pass over these children, because we are unable to address them directly by name.

- *Me and my name:* One simple exercise that you could use at the start of the year is to ask your children to write or talk about their names. If done as a writing task, you might set this as an individual activity, whereas if used as a speaking and listening task, the children could work in small groups. This exercise allows you to use repetition (see above) and also gives you the chance to walk around the classroom, seeing or hearing the students' names over and over again. You might get them started on this exercise by setting them some or all of the following questions:
  - *'What is your name?'*
  - *'How did you get this name? Who gave it to you?'*
  - *'Is there some special meaning or connection attached to your name? For instance, are you named after a relative or a place that is particularly important to your family?'*
  - *'Do you like your name?'*

- o *'If you do, why do you like it?'*
- o *'If you don't, what would you prefer to be called?'*
- o *'Do you have any middle names? If yes, what are these and how do you feel about them?'*
- o *'What does your name say about you? Does it fit well with your personality?*
- o *'What country does your name come from?'*
- o *'Do you know what your name means?'* (If you have it available, a dictionary of names will tell you the meaning of most of the names you encounter.)

- *Visual approaches:* Making names visual is a good way to help yourself retain them. Creating pictures or other images offers the teacher a way to see names on a regular basis. For instance, you might get your children to create a name plate for their desks, or you could get the whole class to make name pictures to put up on your wall. Another visual approach is to use a seating plan. If you decide to do this, and your children are old enough, let them help out, perhaps by each adding a small picture of themselves beside their names. If you have a digital camera, an excellent idea is to take photos of each student, and to create a chart of the class with the children's pictures attached.

- *Name games:* There are lots of name games that you could play with your children to assist you in learning their names. Many of these are a staple of the drama studio but are easily adapted to the 'normal' classroom. You can find a description of several different name games in my book *How to Survive your First Year in Teaching*, or in any good drama book.

Memory system for names

As we saw earlier in this chapter, there are specific strategies or systems that you can use in order to improve your memory. When you're aiming to remember names, the key point to consider is how you might make the connections that are so vital in this pursuit. The idea is to create links between the name you wish to recall and the person to whom that name is attached. Here is an outline of how you can do this:

- On first meeting a child, pick out the most obvious features of his or her face, or other body characteristics that are particularly striking. Consider the following areas.
  o Hair – is this particularly long or short, or is the style especially flat or spiky?
  o Face shape – is the shape of the child's face rounded or long, chubby or slim?
  o Ears – are these a prominent feature, are they large or do they stick out?
  o Eyebrows – are these thick and bushy, thin and wispy, fair or dark?
  o Eyes – are they a striking colour, or do they have an unusual shape?
  o Nose – is this prominent on the face, or does the child have an atypical profile?
  o Mouth – are the lips particularly thick or thin, is the student a smiler, with dimples, or a misery guts, with a downturned mouth?
  o Face 'furniture' – does the child wear glasses, have spots, or anything else on his or her face that stands out?
  o Body – is he or she especially tall or short, fat or thin, or is the child's body shape noticeable for some reason?
- Now consider the child's name, and how you might find a link which allows you to relate this to the striking characteristics which you have identified. To do this, use any of the strategies described in this chapter, such as finding rhymes, using the first thought that pops into your mind, creating large images, and so on. To give a few examples of how this can be done, here are some links with some fairly common names:
  o *Ben:* Ben is built like the proverbial brick house. Consequently, you might create a link in your mind with Big Ben.
  o *Anita:* You teach a child called Anita who has a particularly prominent mouth, and is rather well covered. You choose to link her name with the similar sounding phrase 'an eater', and visualize her stuffing her huge mouth with food.
  o *Harry:* Names that have some type of royal or celebrity connection are easy. Picture any Harrys in your class in full

royal regalia, wearing a crown and sitting on a throne. (Alternatively, you could use the Harry Potter books to create your link.)

o *Jessica:* This one's a bit harder, as it doesn't really bring any images straight to mind, and it doesn't rhyme particularly well with any other words. When you come across more difficult names, you will need to be a little more inventive. With the name Jessica, if the child was blonde you could use *Shooting Stars with Reeves and Mortimer* as the basis for the link. One of the catchphrases on this TV programme is 'Ulrika-ka-ka'. Hear the name as 'Jessica-ca-ca', and create a link between the two in your mind.

– Once you've worked out your name–child connections, take some time to fix the image or thought in your mind, picturing or hearing the name and its link over and over again.

– This process will take a little while to complete with a whole class, so you might aim to remember a limited number of names in each lesson, perhaps five or so.

Memory games and exercises

There are lots of different memory exercises that you can use in your classroom to help you develop your students' memories. These exercises are not only useful in developing the ability to remember, but they are also good fun and a useful way of showing your class how the techniques involved in memory systems work. You can find a couple of examples of memory games for you to try out with your classes described below.

An interesting approach to use with these exercises is to first try them before you do any work on memory. Once you have taught the children some of the skills or techniques involved in remembering, you can then try the exercises again to see the difference. The number link system described earlier in this chapter is fairly easily to learn, and can make a significant difference to the results. Your children will hopefully be amazed at how much better they do after learning a few simple techniques.

Kim's game

Kim's game is a well-known memory exercise that I'm sure the majority of you will have played when you were children. The game works as follows:

- Place a number of different objects on a tray. These could be anything at all that you have to hand – a matchbox, a pen, a coloured cube, and so on.
- Show the tray of objects to the class, and give them a short period of time in which to remember. Two minutes is about the right length of time.
- Remove or cover up the objects.
- Ask the children to list as many of the objects as they can, again in a short space of time.
- Bring back the tray and ask the students to check how many of the objects they were able to remember.

Once you have tried Kim's game with the children, spend some time on showing them how the number link system works. Repeat the exercise, this time with the children using this system, to see whether it helps them to remember more items. You might even like to use this for some maths or science work, comparing the results. Do note that it will probably take your children some time before they are able to create the links quickly.

Variations

There are lots of different ways in which you can vary Kim's game to add more interest to the exercise. Here are a couple of ideas to get you started:

- *What's missing?* Follow the game as described above, but before you bring back the tray remove one object from it. Now ask the class to try and identify which item has been removed.
- *Create a story:* A fictional element will help to make the exercise more interesting and engaging for the children. For instance, you might tell the class that they are going to be working as

detectives, looking at some clues. You could then put the objects in a handbag and get the children to take the items out one at a time to study them. After they have memorized them, again remove one item. The class must try to work out what has been 'stolen'.

Who's missing?

This drama game makes a wonderful exercise in memory and it is also good for developing your children's focus and concentration. It is particularly useful if played near the start of the first term, when the children are getting to know each other. However, it can be played at any time of the year, especially with secondary school classes who do not usually work together. Here's how it works:

- Choose a volunteer to be blindfolded. He or she will be responsible for working out 'who's missing'.
- Ask the children to raise their hands if they would like to go 'missing'. Pick out one student by pointing at him or her. This student leaves the room and stands outside the door.
- If the children are seated, get them to swop places so the 'missing' student isn't immediately obvious by the empty seat. Alternatively, if you have the space, you can have the class standing up.
- Take the blindfold off the volunteer. The child must now work out who is standing outside the room.

Memory and revision

When examination time comes round, having a highly developed memory really pays dividends. For many subjects, being able to memorize certain elements of the curriculum is vital in doing well in an exam. Your students might be memorizing historical facts, points to be made about a set text in literature, steps to be taken in a science experiment, and so on. By teaching your students the tips for remembering given in this chapter, you will certainly give them a head start when it comes to doing well in their exams. The advice below will give you some additional ideas about how to aid your students in their revision.

Approaching revision

For many of our students, the thought of having to revise for exams can cause a great deal of stress. If they do not have any thinking strategies in place to aid them, the tendency will be to simply read a piece of text over and over again, in the hope that some of it will stick. By sharing with your children some explicit strategies and techniques, you can give them the confidence that they will be able to retain much more of what they study. Here are some tips about memory and revision for you to share with them.

- *Keep it short:* Do stress to your class the importance of not trying to revise for too long at any one sitting. We tend to remember most from the start and finish of a period of revision, and less from the central section. Explain this to the children and encourage them to keep their revision periods short – around 20 minutes at a time is about right.
- *Practise recall:* After studying a subject, it is important to check which parts have 'stuck' and which need further work. Encourage your students to test themselves during their revision, to find out what they have actually retained. As I pointed out earlier in this chapter, it is a very good idea to focus on those things that we find most difficult to recall. By testing their own memory processes, your students can work out which parts of the revision need further work.
- *Create structures:* Explain to your class how they should go about structuring their revision. For many of them, this will not be immediately obvious, and they will tend to simply read through the material over and over again. Consequently, the teacher needs to explain exactly how different structures might be used. This might be through the use of plans, diagrams, memory maps, and so on.
- *Create links:* Once they have designed these structures, your students should then go on to create the links and connections

that are needed for retention, for instance, making up their own mnemonics. You can find an explanation of how to do this below.

Creating structures

Because of the way in which our brains work, it is important for our students to learn how to create structures with which to revise. Once these structures have been formed, the students can then move on to memorize their revision notes. This might involve the use of brainstorms, mind maps, diagrams, and so on. When it comes to memorizing the information, the word at the centre of each diagram can be used to spark off a series of other words, that in turn link to words within each brainstorm. You can show your students how to find a way in which to retain these words, for instance by making up mnemonics, as explained below.

Probably the best way to show you how this approach works is to give you an example of the method in action. Say, for instance, that the student has been set the task of writing an essay on the Shakespeare play *Romeo and Juliet* in his or her exam. There might be various themes from the play that would need to be memorized along with information and quotes on each theme. Here is the process that students could undertake to help jog their memory in the exam.

- Create a series of brainstorms that summarize the relevant information. In the example given, the first few of these might look something like the diagram on the opposite page.
- Now take the central words from each brainstorm, and find a way of remembering them. So, the student would have the following start to his or her list:
  o Fate
  o Time
  o Light and dark
- One good way to retain these words is through the use of a mnemonic. If we take the first letters of each word, this gives us F, T and L. (It is probably safe to ignore the D, as this should

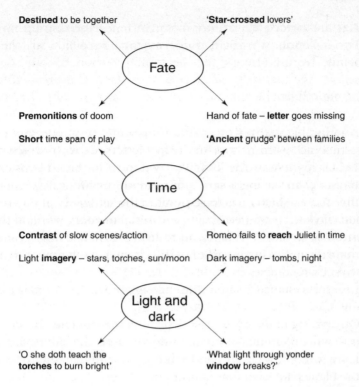

come quickly to the student's mind once he or she sees the word 'light'.) One option for these letters might be the word **FOOTBALL**.

- Next, take one word from each of the points within the brainstorms. In the example given, the words that I would choose have been highlighted in bold. So, we have:
  - o Destined
  - o Star-crossed
  - o Premonitions
  - o Letter
  - o Short
  - o Ancient
  - o Contrast
  - o Reach
  - o Imagery
  - o Torches
  - o Window

- Again, there are various options for remembering this. For instance, we might form a story in which all these words feature. Here's the beginning section of one such story: *'She was destined to be a star, she had a premonition about it. When the letter arrived, it was short, as short as a letter could be . . .'*
- Another alternative is to make up a sentence or sentences in which each word starts with the first letters of the words above. This helps give us the links that we need for better memory. Rather than having a series of random, unconnected words, the student simply has to remember the sentences. It's a great idea if you can connect this to the initial memory word, in this instance 'football'. When you're using this approach, bear in mind the points made earlier in this chapter about how to make things memorable.
- Here, the football-related sentence might be: *'David says play low shots and cross right into the wall.'*
- On arriving in the exam, the first thing the students should do is to write their memory joggers down: here, the letters 'd, s, p, l, s, a, c, r, i, t, w'. They can then use these to help them 'fill in the blanks' for each brainstorm.

6

Critical thinking

When I was writing this book, I had to make some difficult decisions about how to organize the information that I wished to include. At first I had planned to use a division between logical and creative thinking, but one of the problems with this is the fact that so much thought requires a combination of the two approaches. In the end, as you'll see, I've decided to group a number of skills under the term 'critical thinking'. All these skills involve some sort of search to make sense of the world in which we live. They use approaches such as analysis and hypothesizing to examine what already exists, in an effort to establish what is true or correct. In contrast, 'creative thinking', as covered in the next chapter, has the aim of creating something new and original, whether this is an idea, an object, a piece of art, and so on. You'll see that I have also devoted an entire chapter to the issue of working with ideas, as these represent a rather different area, in which the search is for something far more subjective and personal when it comes to establishing the 'truth'.

In this chapter I have included skills such as applying logic, reasoning, hypothesizing, problem solving, information processing and evaluation. Each of these types of thought requires the application of a rational, questioning approach in order to be successful. Traditionally, in the Western world this analytical style is one of the most highly developed and highly valued areas of thinking, and this is perhaps particularly so within schools. Our education system encourages critical thinking across all the subjects, and the examinations which our children sit during their school careers stress the importance of analytical approaches. Whilst I have no quarrel with the value of effective critical thought, I would argue that the balance has perhaps tipped too far in one direction and that we also need to give focus to more creative approaches.

In this chapter you will find lots of advice about teaching the various areas of critical thinking to your children. This includes ideas for exercises in logic and advice about how to develop your students' reasoning, as well as some really engaging approaches to problem solving and mysteries, and also some tips about how to get your class working effectively on information processing and evaluations.

What is critical thinking?

As we saw above, the term 'critical thinking' describes an approach to thinking, rather than one specific thinking skill. The effective critical thinker employs a number of different techniques during the thinking process. Coming to a definition of critical thinking is actually quite hard, because the term encompasses such a wide variety of features. Here are some ideas about the different approaches that a good critical thinker would use.

- *Searching:* The aim of the critical thinker is to make a logical assessment of the world in which we live, in a search for what is true and correct. He or she undertakes a hunt for ways of understanding ideas, theories, situations, and so on. In the process of this search, changes and additions are made to the thinker's understanding of the world.
- *Analysing:* During the critical thinker's search, a number of different analytical techniques are put into action. This might mean asking questions, analysing any confusions, making judgements, finding what is relevant, and so on. The process of analysing is a very active one in which the critical thinker interacts dynamically with the material.
- *Proposing:* As part of the process of searching and analysing, the critical thinker will put forward or propose ideas, making

statements about what he or she believes to be true. The technique of proposing encompasses areas such as reasoning and hypothesizing, which are covered in more detail further on in this chapter.

- *Connecting:* Making connections is, in my opinion, one of the most important thinking skills of all. The effective critical thinker is able to look for and find connections between different ideas, to show how these connections work, and to use them to further his or her thinking.
- *Solving:* In addition to proposing and coming to reasoned conclusions, we can also use critical thinking to solve problems or to find answers to issues that we face. The critical thinker makes looking for solutions an integral part of his or her search.
- *Supporting:* When thinking critically, we must find evidence to support the statements that we make or the beliefs that we hold. This process of finding proof to support our conclusions is crucial in the development of more complex thinking, for instance, when writing essays.
- *Testing:* An important step in the search for what is true is the willingness to test out the statements we make or the ideas we propose. The critical thinker must look for weaknesses in his or her reasoning or in what has been created. This skill is particularly evident in areas such as hypothesizing and evaluating.
- *Maintaining objectivity:* During the process of critical thinking, we must learn to rely on reason rather than emotion. The aim must be to find the best explanation, rather than to focus on being 'right'. In the goal of maintaining objectivity, the thinker might check for motives and bias, or recognize his or her prejudices about the subject in question.
- *Being disciplined:* Thinking effectively means taking a comprehensive, exhaustive approach to a task. This might mean finding all possible evidence, and refusing to ignore any evidence that doesn't fit within our initial proposal. We must also aim to be as precise and clear as possible in the way that we put forward our ideas.
- *Being open-minded:* Finally, the critical thinker needs to be open to all interpretations, studying any number of viewpoints, rather than being limited to a single position. As far as possible,

we should approach any material with caution, asking for proof and keeping an open, sceptical attitude to what we are told.

Looking at logic

A very simple definition of logic would be 'a search for what is true', and this means it plays a vital part in critical thinking. When we are looking for what is logical, we are aiming to find out what must be true of necessity – what cannot be anything else but true, taking all the facts and circumstances into consideration. We must ensure that the information on which we base our logic is fully worked out and that there are no other factors that could potentially be involved. To give an example, I might make an apparently logical statement such as: *'Ben has two parents, one is his mother, so logically the other must be his father.'* On the surface of it, this statement is completely logical and true. However, it fails to take into consideration the fact that there are various possible definitions of 'parents'. For instance, it could be that Ben has been adopted by two women who are both legally considered to be his parents.

At its most basic level, being logical simply means taking a completely sensible and rational approach to any question, problem or activity. For instance, creating a logical sequence involves putting actions or events into the order in which they must go, if the whole process is going to work. Putting forward a logical statement means following what is rational to its conclusion. Often, these supposedly logical statements can seem rather stupid, as in: *'My cat is black and white. Cows are black and white. Therefore my cat is a cow.'* Although this statement is, on the surface of it, completely logical, it fails to take into account the background information that actually makes it a nonsense, such as:

- many different animals are coloured black and white;
- cats and cows come in all different colours, not just black and white.

120

To summarize, logic is what appears to make sense, but if this is in the absence of certain information, then the logic falls apart. Consequently, when helping our children to learn how to take a logical approach, we must ensure that they consider all the different factors that could apply to the situation. Although logic is very much a left-brain activity, our children actually need to use the right sides of their brains and to be creative in their responses to what appears to be logical on the surface. Working on logic is an excellent way of encouraging our students to develop rational arguments, because it requires them to look at all the different factors that need to be considered.

Exercises in logic

When you're teaching thinking skills to your students, there are a whole range of different exercises in logic that you can use. As well as simply working on these activities, it is also an excellent idea to talk about the different thought processes that take place in the mind as they are completed. Below, I give a variety of logic exercises that you could use with your children to develop this area of thinking. These exercises are designed to explore a variety of different forms in which logic plays a part.

Is it logical?

Give your children a scenario to work with, and ask them to search for what is logical and true within this situation. I've given one example below to get you started. This suggestion takes place within the school setting, but you could come up with further scenarios from the world at large. When you are devising your storyline, aim to make the information given appear to fit only one version of events, so that your children are forced to be as creative as they can be in their search for other possible truths.

You see Nicola and Jessica talking secretly in a corner of the playground. Nicola is known to be the class bully; Jessica is a very quiet and timid girl. As you watch you can see that Nicola appears to be angry,

> *while Jessica looks frightened and is crying. As they finish talking, you see Jessica hand over some coins to Nicola. You think that Nicola has been bullying Jessica, and threatening her so that she gives her money. Is this a logical conclusion? Is it the only possible conclusion? Should you tell a teacher about what you have witnessed, or should you confront Nicola to find out her side of the story?*

Although the assumption reached would, on the surface of it, appear to be completely logical, there are in fact a number of other potential conclusions. As we established above, it is essential to be in possession of all the facts before we can come to a logical answer. In this case the witness has only what he or she has seen to go on, and there are actually a number of options. Your children will need to be as creative as possible in their search for other possibilities, and in their hunt for what could potentially be true. Here are some other logical answers.

- Nicola and Jessica are actually good friends. Nicola lent Jessica some money ages ago, and has now asked for it back, because she needs to buy her mum a birthday present. Jessica is crying because she only has half the money and cannot pay her friend back. Nicola is angry, because she feels that her friend has let her down.
- Jessica has stolen some money from the teacher's purse. Nicola saw her doing this, and she is insisting that Jessica returns it. Jessica is terrified that she is going to get into trouble, and this is why she is crying. Eventually, Nicola offers to return the money herself and Jessica hands it over.

There are various approaches to this exercise. You might get the children working on the scenario, individually, in pairs or perhaps in larger groups. After they have spent some time discussing the problem, you could then pull the class together to hear the different opinions. As an alternative, or as a way of developing this exercise further, you could ask your children to act out their conclusions, showing the different possible truths within this scenario. The students might show you scenes in which:

- Nicola is confronted by some of her classmates;
- the witnesses go to a teacher to say what they have seen;
- Nicola and Jessica are questioned by another child.

Language and logic

In this exercise the students are given a complex sentence and asked to find the answer within a set period of time. It's a good idea to make the time limit a short one, to get the children working with focus. The difficulty in this exercise is actually working out what is meant, searching for the true and logical meaning within the words. By using complex sentences, you can encourage your children to really get their thinking going. For instance, you might give them a statement which has a variety of possible answers, and which contains the use of double negatives. It is particularly difficult for the mind to work out double negatives because we have to contain a number of 'non-thoughts' in our heads at the same time. Here's an example of a question that requires a logical approach to find the solution.

> *The answer to this question is either 1, 2, 3 or 4. If the Earth is not round, then the answer is not 1, 2 or 3. If the sun is not a star, then the answer is either 1 or 3. If the last word in this question is 'out', then the answer is 2. Can you work it out?*

The skill here is having to hold a series of points in your head at one time in order to come to a logical conclusion. The use of the double negatives 'not round' and 'not 1, 2 or 3' makes it more difficult for the students to sustain the answer in their heads. In fact, the final point actually allows them to work out the answer without having to look at the whole question, but they must realize this and follow the logic.

Odd one out

This simple classifying and sorting exercise requires the children to take a logical approach to the information that they have been given. They must consider the various elements that are particular to the items given, and then find logical connections between them, in order to work out which one does not fit. It is worth noting that in many instances your students may choose an item that is different from the one you had anticipated, finding different yet equally logical connections and links. For instance, you might have the series:

- horse
- cat
- dog
- bird

In this case, 'bird' would appear to be the 'odd one out', as it is the only animal that can fly, and it is also the only one of these animals which has two legs rather than four. However, your students might suggest 'horse' as a logical alternative, as it is the only animal in the list that a person can ride. A more difficult example might be:

- kettle
- puddle
- sink
- saucepan

In this example, your children may well choose 'puddle', pointing out that this is the only item not found in a kitchen. Another logical answer could be 'saucepan', because this is the only one that does not normally contain water. In fact, you may well find the value of this exercise to be more within the thinking that it throws up, rather than in finding the 'correct' answers. Some very interesting discussion work could lead on from these 'odd one out' exercises about the nature and meaning of logic.

Following instructions

The following exercise can be easily adapted to a whole host of topics or curriculum subjects where the use of instructions is required. For instance, you might give a series of instructions for a science experiment, or a list of directions for doing long division. To do this exercise, ask the children to put the instructions below into the most logical order, using the skill of sequencing to do so.

Making scrambled eggs
- add a dash of milk to the eggs;
- switch on the cooker ring;
- break the eggs;
- put the pan on the ring to heat;
- assemble the ingredients and equipment;
- whisk the eggs and milk together;
- pour the egg and milk mixture into the pan;
- add a knob of butter to the pan;
- whisk the mixture as it cooks.

Discussion points
After completing the exercise, you might like to talk with your children about the mental processes involved, and also the different logical approaches that could potentially be taken. Here are some discussion points to guide you:

- *'How did you work out the order in which to put the instructions?'*
- *'Can the instructions be put into more than one logical order?'*
- *'Is it possible to change the order, and for the recipe still to work?'*
- *'How can this be done, and why will the instructions still work?'*
- *'Did everyone come up with the same order? If not, why not?'*

As a follow-up activity, once the children have decided on the logical order in which to follow the instructions, you might actually get them to make the scrambled eggs. They could try this out using one order of instructions, then test out various different sequences to see whether each one works equally well.

Hypothesizing

Hypothesizing is closely linked to logic: when we come up with a hypothesis we are aiming to find a theory or a premise that is 'true'. In order to create a hypothesis, a series of known (or assumed) facts, concepts, deductions or thoughts are put together to come to a possible theory, or 'working thought'. The theory that is found must be correct and logical in a specific situation, and it is important that it is tested out to validate (or disprove) its accuracy. The aim is to try to prove it to be wrong, making sure that all the facts fit with the theory as it stands. If they do not, then the hypothesis is not logical. The testing that is carried out should ensure that the hypothesis is accurate, factually correct, or that it works, as in the case of an invention or a scientific idea. In Chapter 8, which deals with creativity, I look at the area of speculation. Hypothesis and speculation are closely linked, with speculation being a rather more imaginative and creative way of going about a similar exercise. Speculation allows the imagination to roam reasonably free, but hypothesizing means taking a logical path to a possible truth.

Hypothesizing is found in many walks of life and in the classroom is perhaps particularly useful in the teaching of science, although this is by no means its only application. Learning how to create a logical hypothesis helps our children develop a number of important thinking skills, including the ability to reason and to give evidence to support their proposals. One situation in which hypothesizing is commonly found outside of school is in the problem solving approach used by detectives to solve crimes. You can find some ideas about how you might use this in the section below on 'Working with mysteries'. Below are a couple of exercises that could be used with your students to work on developing their ability to hypothesize.

Where's Teddy?

This exercise requires the children to come to a hypothesis, using the information that they have been given. Ask them to create a logical theory about what might have happened to Teddy, and to give reasons to back up the conclusions they reach. They must ensure that they account for all the pieces of evidence that they have been given.

Teddy has gone missing. When you search his room you find some clues to help you locate him. These are:

- the bedroom door is locked;
- the window has been broken from the outside;
- there are large muddy footprints on the floor;
- these footprints are too big to have been made by Teddy;
- one of Teddy's suitcases is missing;
- all of Teddy's savings have gone.

In response to this scenario, one child might propose the following theory:

I think Teddy has been kidnapped. I think this because the window was broken from the outside, so somebody might have come into his room and stolen him. Also, the mud on the floor tells me that somebody else has entered the room.

However, in this instance, the child has not accounted for the missing money and suitcase. Another child might suggest a different hypothesis:

I think Teddy has run away with a friend. He was locked in his room and this friend came to rescue him. The friend had to break open the window in order to let Teddy out, because the door was locked and he was trapped inside. Teddy packed a suitcase and took all his money with him to help on his journey.

Why do? / Why is? / Why are?

This activity asks the students to come up with reasonable hypotheses in response to a series of 'why do?', 'why is?' and 'why are?' questions. These are the sort of questions that many young children puzzle over. They are perhaps particularly useful in incorporating thinking skills into science lessons. However, it should be possible for you to adapt the specific questions that you ask to the relevant area of the curriculum being taught. Here are some examples of questions to get you started.

- *'Why do cats have whiskers?'*
- *'Why do we only see the moon at night time?'*
- *'Why do flowers come in lots of different colours?'*
- *'Why do people and animals need to sleep?'*
- *'Why is the sky blue?'*
- *'Why is coal black?'*
- *'Why are there 24 hours in a day?'*
- *'Why are babies born without teeth?'*

Once the children have come up with a suggested hypothesis in answer to the questions you pose, they should then move on to test whether their theory is correct, accurate and logical. One way of approaching this activity is to ask an individual to propose a hypothesis to the class, and then ask the rest of the students to try and prove it wrong. The child who has put forward his or her theory must use thinking skills to defend the suggestion against all possible counterarguments.

Reasoning

Reasoning is the process whereby we make inferences that go beyond what we already know. There are various ways in which we can come to these inferences, including the application of logic, intuition, creativity, and so on. When we reason, we take a piece or pieces of information, analyse them, come to some assumptions about them, and then use these deductions in some way. Reasoning helps us to make sense of the world in which we live, and also to lead a safe and effective life.

We spend our lives in a constant process of reasoning. Almost every minute of the day we are coming to reasoned judgements about what we should or should not do. The judgements that we make might be conscious or subconscious, as we calculate different factors or try to interpret a situation in the hope of making the right decision. For instance, you might apply reasoning to decide whether to drive or cycle to school. In this situation you would need to take into consideration factors such as traffic, weather conditions, costs, safety, and so on.

When applied in an academic context, reasoning is the method whereby we construct a logical argument, analysing the information that we have in order to make reasoned statements about a subject. As part of the process, we must give explanations to support the statements we make. We must also look for any possible weaknesses or faults in our reasoning. Reasoning plays an important role in many subjects, and is particularly vital when it comes to writing essays. Here are some tips for teaching your children how to reason effectively.

- *Clarify the issue:* Before they begin the task of reasoning, it is important that our students identify the issue at hand. They can do this by posing themselves a clear and simple question to answer. In the example given above about travelling to work, the issue is about the preferred mode of transport between only two different choices. In this case the question set might be: *'Is it better for me to travel to school by car or by bicycle?'* This question will help to focus the reasoning so that it deals only with what is relevant in the specific situation. Alternative questions along similar, but subtly different, lines might include: *'Is it cheaper for me to travel to school by car or by bicycle?'* or *'What is the best method by which to travel to school?'*
- *Give supporting ideas and evidence:* It is important that our children learn how to support the reasoned statements that they make. This ability becomes particularly crucial when they are learning how to construct essays and make complex arguments. A good way to start your children providing supporting evidence for their reasoning is to give them a simple framework within which to propose their ideas. This might be as straightforward as: *'I think x because x.'* By using this format they will be forced to give a considered reason for every statement. This idea is developed further in my book *Getting the Buggers to Write*, in which I write about a four-step process for writing essays. This process asks the students to go through the following steps in creating an argument: statement – evidence – explanation – development. You can also find some more thoughts about this approach in Chapter 8 of this book, in the section on developing arguments.

- *Consider objective/subjective reasoning:* Human beings are not always entirely logical and so our reasoning can easily be influenced by the prejudices or preferences that we hold. If we are aiming to reason objectively, it is important that we work hard to make our reasoning as impartial as possible. Alternatively, we might choose to take into account our personal feelings during the reasoning process and to take a more subjective approach to the question at hand. For instance, in the example given about travelling to work, it could be that the person considering this question hates getting wet. Consequently, he or she might focus more on the benefits of car driving, simply to avoid the need to cycle to work in the rain. Of course, this personal preference could be put forward as a reason for choosing the car over the bicycle. In this case the reasoning would tend more towards the subjective than the objective.

- *View it from all sides:* When we are trying to take a rational, logical approach in our reasoning, it is important that we learn to view the situation from all sides. We can do this by stepping outside our own responses to the question, and considering the wider implications of the arguments we present. It is a good idea to try out our reasoning by considering how different people might respond in the same situation. This will help us reason as fully and completely as possible. In the transport example given, we might consider the reasons for cycling that an environmentalist would give, such as the environmental costs of using a car over a bicycle. We could also examine the reasoning that a parent would use to persuade his or her child that being driven to school is the best choice, such as arguments about the potential dangers of cycling.

- *View it as a process:* Reasoning is very much a moving process rather than a static event. As they reason, our students should aim to keep an open mind, rather than coming to a decision part of the way through. At its best, reasoning should enable us to change our minds several times during the process and only decide on a final viewpoint once we have examined all the information available.

- *Apply the correct structures:* It is important that we apply the correct structures so that our reasoning makes sense. For instance, this might mean applying the accepted rules of addition or division to a maths question. Without these rules or structures, what seems at first glance to be 'reasonable' may well be completely incorrect.

- *Come to a conclusion:* At the end of the reasoning process, we need to come to an overall conclusion. By demonstrating the finished outcome of the deductions we have made, we can complete the argument that we have created.

The personnel managers' dilemma

This is an excellent exercise that uses reasoning skills and that the students find highly engaging. I have used it very successfully with students at secondary level, but you should be able to simplify or adapt it so that it works from the early years of primary school as well. For instance, you might use the same format to create an exercise called 'Who shall we have on our team?' in which the children have to decide from a number of different candidates for a school sports team. Or, if you're brave enough, you might set an exercise entitled 'Who do we want as our teacher?' For this activity you could give the children a list of potential teachers and ask them to choose the one that will be best for them, giving reasons for the choice that they make.

The personnel managers' dilemma uses the same form as the 'role of the expert' activity described earlier, and consequently the organizational tips given in that section will also apply here. In this particular situation, the students are acting as 'expert' personnel managers. Here's an explanation of how to run this activity.

- Create a company, choosing a name and also deciding on the product that your company makes. (This can be the generic 'widget' if you don't want to be too specific.)
- Make up a number of different workers and type out their information for the personnel managers to consider. Include details such as:
  o job title;
  o salary (this might be a fixed amount, or basic plus commission for sales staff);

- o benefits (such as company car);
- o length of service;
- o assessment reports;
- o personal circumstances;
- o personality.
- Explain to your class that the company is experiencing financial difficulties, and consequently needs to find a way to lower costs. The managing director has suggested that staff cuts would be a good way of saving money and has asked the personnel department to come up with a list of candidates for redundancy. Set a specific amount of money that must be saved – for instance, £50,000.
- Tell your students that it is entirely up to them how they go about saving the money. They will need to report back to the managing director on their findings and it is important that they are able to give valid reasons for the decisions that they make. (Note: in my experience, many of the children go straight for the idea of sacking staff. However, some students do pick up on the idea that there might be other ways of saving money, for instance, by doing away with company cars, and so on.)
- Split the class up into groups of personnel managers, and hand out the candidate details to each group. The students must then hold a meeting at which they discuss the different candidates, and decide how to go about reducing costs. They must come up with a reasoned proposal to present to the managing director. You might choose to have this delivered verbally or you could ask your students to make a written report.
- During the exercise, you can add in various pieces of information, particularly if the students are not considering all the angles. For instance, you might drop in the news that redundancy pay is dependent on length of service. Alternatively, you could get the class researching to get any background information that they require.
- After the reports have been made, an interesting extension activity is to ask your students to act out meetings with the staff they have chosen to sack. This helps them understand the impact that losing a job could have on someone and makes the exercise less about abstract reasoning.

Problem solving

Just as with reasoning, problem solving is a crucial part of our everyday lives. By equipping our children to solve the problems that they face, we not only develop their work within the classroom, but we also help prepare them for coping with the world outside the school gates. The posing of problems and the finding of ways to solve them is a hugely satisfying activity. To be as successful as possible at solving problems, we need to apply a combination of logic and creativity.

When teaching your students about problem solving, there are four basic steps that should prove helpful.

- *Identification of the problem:* The first step is to identify exactly what the problem is that needs solving. This is not necessarily as straightforward as it sounds. For instance, in the alarm clock example given below, we might be tempted to identify the problem as a broken alarm clock. However, the specific problem that actually needs solving is the difficulty in getting up on time for school. By identifying the problem at hand, we avoid becoming sidetracked into a single line of thought, without looking for alternatives. If we focused solely on fixing the alarm clock this might prevent us from seeing that there are in fact a number of different possible approaches that might be taken. Much depends on the viewpoint we choose to take, and in fact with some issues we might come up with a number of different potential 'problems'. For example, in the scenario below about buying a birthday present, the problem might be identified as a lack of money (resulting in a search for ways to make some cash). Alternatively, the issue could be seen as the need to give a present, and this might lead us to some very different solutions.
- *Devising potential solutions:* When we are looking for potential solutions, we have the chance to apply both logical and creative thinking. Our first response might be to look for the most logical answers to the problem, and one of these might well be exactly what we need. However, if we can also apply some creative or lateral thinking, this will help us find ways of

coming at the problem from more original angles. As you can see in the 'buying a toy' example below, the application of some lateral thinking comes up with the suggestion of making the present rather than paying for it.

- *Testing the solutions:* Once we have found a number of different solutions to the problem, we then need to check their usefulness. The first consideration is whether a specific solution is actually possible in the circumstances. Secondly, we need to identify which one from a number of different possibilities is the most likely to work. Finally, we need to establish which of our solutions will work the best. We can do all this by testing them out. Depending on the particular situation, this testing might be done either by actually trying the solutions, or alternatively simply by thinking about or discussing the factors involved and working out the most suitable approach.
- *Making a choice:* When the testing process has been completed we can then make a choice about which solution to use and actually put this into action. Sometimes, we will make a decision and then discover that the solution is not as effective as we had hoped. In this instance, we should feel free to throw away the decision and start over again, trying out a different answer.

Here are a few problems, and some potential solutions, that you might like to work on with your students.

- You want to buy a toy for your friend's birthday, but you don't have enough money.
- Here are some ideas that your students might propose:
  o earn some extra money by finding a job;
  o borrow some money from your parents;
  o choose a different present that doesn't cost so much;
  o gang together with another friend so that you can afford to buy the present;
  o make a present instead, on the premise that a handmade gift demonstrates true friendship;
  o save up for longer, and give the toy as a joint birthday/Christmas present.

- You need to get up on time for school, but your alarm clock is broken.
- You devise a number of different solutions:
  o buy a new alarm clock;
  o fix the old alarm clock;
  o ask your parents to wake you up instead;
  o get a friend to call you in the morning on your mobile phone;
  o sleep with the curtains open, hoping that the light will wake you up;
  o turn up late and give the broken alarm clock as an excuse.

Working with mysteries

Children of all ages (and adults too, of course) absolutely love mysteries. There is a huge sense of excitement in finding clues, examining evidence, and coming up with a logical solution to the puzzle that faces us. When we ask our students to look for logical links between a clue and a suspect, or between a crime and a range of possible motives, they are forced to use a variety of different thinking skills. Solving mysteries will, of course, assist us in developing reasoning skills, problem solving, and rational thinking. In addition, it will also help us to develop our children's imagination, because often a good dose of creativity is required in finding possible but more unusual solutions.

We can use mysteries in a wide variety of formats to develop our children's thinking skills. Below you'll find two ideas to get you started, but the really great thing about mysteries is that there are as many different ideas as the teacher's imagination can devise. When you're working on solving a mystery with your class, it is useful to spend some time discussing some of the thinking issues involved. Here are some discussion points to get you started.

- *'Is there always one "right" solution to a mystery?'*
- *'Can we find a number of possible solutions?'*
- *'Is the most logical solution always the correct one?'*
- *'What is the role of creative thought in solving mysteries?'*

- *'How can we test out a solution or hypothesis to find out whether it is right?'*

The genre of crime stories absolutely thrives on mystery, whether in books, on the television or in films. Clues and red herrings abound, and the question of 'whodunnit?' keeps the reader or viewer riveted, desperate to find out how the story will unfold. Below is a description of a lesson, using the crime genre, that you could use when it comes to solving mysteries with your students. As you will see from the cross-curricular nature of the activities, this lesson could be used for a number of different subject areas in either the primary or secondary classroom.

The scene of the crime

For this activity, the children work in role as detectives to solve a murder. Using this approach is absolutely guaranteed to make them engrossed and interested in the work. Trying to deduce what has happened will help develop their logical, reasoning and problem-solving skills, at the same time as allowing them a good splash of creativity and imagination.

- *Setting up:* To begin the exercise, the teacher sets up a scene of the crime in the classroom, using real objects and, if possible, a real person (perhaps a student loaned from another class) to play the victim. This should be done before the lesson begins, so that the scene is ready when the children arrive at the beginning of class. To make the scenario as realistic as possible, fence off this area using coloured tape or rope of some sort to simulate a police line. There is no need to have a particular set of props – I tend to use whatever comes to hand. To give an example, you might have:
  o a table with two hands of cards;
  o two chairs, one of which has been knocked over;
  o coins scattered across the table and the floor;
  o a bottle lying on the floor at the far side of the scene;
  o a computer disk;
  o a piece of paper with 'John' and a number written on it;

o if possible, some disposable light plastic gloves, for handling the evidence.

- *Introduction:* When the children arrive at the classroom, introduce the lesson by telling them that there has been a murder. (At this point, if some of your more delicate souls become scared you can take a moment to explain that the scenario is in fact a fiction.) Tell the class that when they go into the room they should not touch anything beyond the crime scene tape. If you ask them why this is they will probably tell you all about fingerprints and trace evidence!

- *Initial discussion:* The children must work as detectives to try and solve the mystery. The first step is to take a look at the scene and to discuss as a class what might have happened. You could ask for a volunteer to cross the police line and, wearing the gloves, hold up each piece of evidence in turn for the class to discuss.

- *Further activities:* The students might then be split up into groups to come up with a hypothesis. Once they have devised their scenario, they could act this out for the class, using the crime scene as a stage area and involving the props in the story that they tell. You could ask them to provide various details in their hypothesis, including:

o how the crime happened;
o what the murder weapon was;
o what the motive was;
o the order of events;
o the likely perpetrator;
o how he or she could be caught.

Thinking and information

The National Curriculum identifies 'information processing' as an important area of thinking. (I'm not too keen on this term, as it does rather conjure up an image of our students as machines.) When it comes to finding and working with information, we can help our students develop a number of important thinking skills. These include speed reading, note taking, organization, structuring and analysing.

Finding information

We might be finding information to help us with a piece of writing such as a project or essay, or perhaps when revising for an exam. Whatever the reason for the search, undertaking research is an excellent way to develop your students' thinking. Before our students go about finding information, they will need to make some decisions for themselves, or obtain some details from their teacher. This process will assist them in their search and make it more likely that the information found will be relevant. The decision-making process includes:

- identifying exactly why the information is required;
- establishing what the information is needed for;
- considering where the relevant information will be found, for example, in books, on the Internet, by asking an expert, and so on;
- deciding how much information is actually needed;
- thinking about the level of detail that is required;
- establishing how much time is available for the research.

Dealing with written information

When undertaking research via the written word, you have the chance to teach your students some very useful thinking skills. There is no space here for a detailed description of techniques such as speed reading. However, here are some quick tips that you can teach your children about how to deal with written information, whether on the page or the screen.

- *A quick overview:* On first approaching a piece of text, especially if it is long and densely printed, it can be difficult to identify and take in the relevant information. This is where the quick overview will pay dividends. Encourage your students to flick through the piece of text before going on to read it in more detail. They could usefully start this overview by looking at a contents page, if there is one. After they have done this they can speed through the whole text to see how it is structured and to pick out any points that are immediately obvious.

- *Locating key words:* Most of the vocabulary that makes up a piece of text is in fact reasonably superfluous and is only there to ensure that the sentences actually make sense and that they read well. To give an example, in the sentence that you have just read, the key words that contain the nub of what is meant are actually relatively few. In this instance – 'most vocabulary', 'superfluous', 'ensure', 'make sense' and perhaps 'read well'. Aim to teach your children how to locate key words, especially if they are dealing with factual or technical writing. This vocabulary will usually stick out on the page because these tend to be long and less commonly used words. The student can skim through a piece of text to pick out these words, rather than necessarily having to read the information in full detail.
- *Avoid 'sounding out':* When we first learn to read, we are trained to sound out the words in order to understand them and make sense of the text. As reading out loud gives way to reading silently in our heads, many of us continue to sound out words as we read them. However, this approach slows us down in our reading, and in fact is not actually necessary for us to obtain meaning. The ability to drop this mental sounding out speeds up our reading exponentially, and enables us to process information at a much faster speed. You can show your students how this can be done by asking them to skim-read a passage, giving them only a short period of time in which to complete the reading. Follow this up by testing to see how much they have actually understood and retained. This will often be a surprisingly large amount.

Organizing information

In Chapter 4, which deals with structures, you can find some useful ideas about how to organize information. Learning to organize the information we find is important in developing thinking because it requires us to use skills such as sorting, sequencing, ordering, and so on. It is also important so that we are able to access the relevant points at a later stage. If the information that they gather is going to be used for revision, our students will need to format it in such a way that they are able to study it and subsequently recollect it in an exam. If it's going to be used as a set of notes to inform a piece of writing such as an essay, they would need to sort it into the relevant order, grouping together the points to be contained within each paragraph. The process of organization might take place as follows.

- As they read a text, the students make brief notes about important points.
- They then take an overview of these points and look for links between the different ideas.
- The points are sorted into groups, and each group of points is placed into a scattergram.
- They look through the scattergrams to consider the most suitable order in which to format them.

Evaluative thinking

Evaluative thinking is hugely important in our children's learning: it allows them to take stock of where they already are with the work, and hopefully to take some steps forward, improving on what they can already do. The way that you approach evaluation will vary according to the subject that you're teaching. However, there are some general principles that largely hold true right across the curriculum. The sections that follow give you ideas about how to approach evaluative thinking in your own classroom.

Why is evaluative thinking important?

Being able to look critically at our own work, and that of others, is a hugely important part of the learning process. By examining what we are already capable of producing, we undertake the vital process of self-evaluation. The reflection involved in this gives us the opportunity to see where we're making mistakes, to amend these errors, and to move onwards and upwards. Here are some thoughts about why evaluative thinking is so important.

- *Exploring successful approaches:* By asking our children to examine the work that they (and others) have done, we will encourage them to think about what factors go together to create a successful approach in a particular subject or topic area. Once they learn how to explore what works and why, they will hopefully be able to repeat the effective parts and eliminate the less effective in their own work.

- *Emulating standards:* When they look at other pieces of work, whether these are of a professional standard, or simply done by a more able student, this gives our children a benchmark for which to aim. For example, they might be reading a well-written story and evaluating exactly what makes it successful.

- *Copying methods and approaches:* As the saying goes, imitation is the sincerest form of flattery. If other people's ideas and approaches work, then sensible students use these as a basis or template for their own work. By examining and evaluating the methods and approaches used by others, our students can apply the positive aspects of someone else's efforts to their own work.

- *An outside observer:* When we undertake a task such as writing an essay or drawing a picture, we are fully involved with it. This proximity to the work means that it can be hard to look at the results objectively. Our students need to develop the ability to look at their own work dispassionately, standing back and responding as an outside audience would. By practising the skill of evaluation we can teach our children to apply this vital objectivity in their thinking.

- *Testing for success:* The inventor who comes up with an idea for a new machine, and subsequently makes a prototype, must spend time testing it to see whether or not it actually works properly. The same applies to our students. For instance, if they were building a model aeroplane in a design and technology lesson, they would need to evaluate the model to check that it works and whether adaptations could be made that would improve it further.

- *Checking for logic and accuracy:* Evaluation is not just about examining what is 'good' about a piece of work, it is also about ensuring that the work is 'correct'. This means that our students need to learn to check for the logic of what they propose, and also to ensure that it is accurate. This might mean checking for correct spelling and grammar, or ensuring that a series of sums do in fact add up.

How to approach evaluations

One of the main experiences many children have of evaluation is via their teacher's marking, particularly when this marking is detailed and includes evaluative comments designed for the student to make improvements. In this type of marking the teacher points out what works well and why, and also what needs developing, and how this development might be undertaken. In my experience, there can be a tendency towards negativity when children are evaluating their own and each other's work. I'm not entirely sure why this is, but I do wonder whether it comes about as a result of the almost constant testing that takes place in school these days. Excessive assessment is perhaps encouraging our students to see their work as being either right or wrong, and leading them towards the feeling that other people are always aiming to judge what they produce. This negativity can be very destructive to a child's morale, especially for academically weak students, who must feel they are always getting it wrong.

When you are working on evaluations with your class, you have an excellent opportunity to overcome this negative approach in their thinking. You should aim to show your children how high quality, positive evaluations can help us to develop the work that we do in a much more constructive way. In addition, evaluating in an encouraging manner can improve the attitude of the whole class towards their lessons. I give some ideas below about how you could do this. Of course, there are times when it is necessary to pick out the faults and downsides of a piece of work, but I believe we need to balance this with creating a positive attitude to what our children have achieved.

- *Give them a tight structure:* When setting an evaluation task, rather than simply asking the class to evaluate, why not give them a specific structure within which to complete their evaluation?

This will help you focus their work towards a positive appraisal. For instance, you might:

o ask them to find three good points about the work;

o tell them to choose the one most impressive aspect of the piece;

o give them specific points on which to comment in a positive way: for instance, naming one good thing about the way this piece of writing is structured, and one way in which the writer uses his or her imagination well.

- *Rule out negativity:* Alternatively, you can tell your children to pick out only the good points of their own work, or that of someone else. No negative comments are allowed at all. This positive approach in fact forces them to think very carefully about the piece that is being evaluated.

- *Pass it on:* Another idea is to get your children passing their work around the classroom, so that they receive a number of different (positive) evaluative comments. Tell the children that they have only a short time to note one good thing about the piece, and then to pass it on to the next student. This exercise should really boost their confidence, as they see a number of different points made about the good aspects of their work.

So, how exactly do you go about approaching evaluative thinking with your class or classes? Here are some ideas that will help you structure the evaluations done in your lessons, and show you how to make evaluation a positive and interesting part of your work with your children.

- *Think about different formats:* Although the majority of evaluations tend to take place individually, consider whether you might also get the children working as a whole class or in small groups. Remember to use both self evaluation and the evaluation of other people's work. Consider also whether a written, spoken or other format is most appropriate for the particular evaluation. You might want to take into account the potential time involved when you make this decision.

- *Use a framework:* Why not produce a sheet that guides the children in their evaluations, particularly if your students are not old enough to write detailed comments of their own? The sheet might ask for a mark out of ten for various different aspects of the work, or you might use stickers or some other visual way of commenting.

- *Think about when you do it:* We do perhaps tend to focus on evaluation as an activity that takes place at the end of lessons, as an examination of what has been achieved. However, there is no reason at all why it should not be used as part of the process of actually doing the work. In a lesson that has a number of short tasks, you might pause for a few minutes after each one and get the class to make a quick verbal assessment of their work so far. Alternatively, you might start out a lesson with an evaluation of a highly successful piece, for instance an extract from a novel, the work of an A-level student, or a model examination answer. By picking this type of work apart, you can help the children understand the elements that go together to make up an effective response. They will hopefully be able to go on to emulate these in their own work.

- *Think about what you evaluate:* Swopping around work within a class, so that the children evaluate other students' pieces, is an excellent way of developing evaluative skills. In addition, you could swop work between different classes, and even different year groups, so that your children see the level at which others are working. You might also start off a lesson with a 'professional'-standard piece, as described above.

- *Use displays:* Putting a child's work up on display gives a very powerful message about how much you value it. Seeing their classmates' work on the walls also allows the students to make informal evaluations of the standard at which others are working. Try to avoid only putting up polished and academically impressive work – you might have a child whose spelling is not great, but whose work shows wonderful imagination.

Evaluative questions

The following questions provide a basis for evaluating most types of work across the curriculum. Some of the questions will apply more often to some subjects than to others. For instance, the question *'Is it correct?'* will be particularly applicable to the more technical subjects such as maths, where many questions have right and wrong answers. Similarly, evaluating whether a piece appeals to the correct audience would tend to be about written tasks.

- *'Does it make sense?'*
- *'Is it correct?'*
- *'What is good about it and why do these things make it good?'*
- *'What is bad about it and why do these things not work?'*
- *'Is it well written?'*
- *'Does it appeal to the audience it's aimed at?'*
- *'Is it easy to understand, but not too simplistic?'*
- *'Is it interesting and engaging, will it hold the attention?'*
- *'Is it properly structured, and easy to follow what is being said?'*
- *'Does it have the correct or proper layout for the topic it covers?'*
- *'Is anything missing from the work?'*
- *'Are the points made developed properly?'*

7

Creative thinking

As an English and drama teacher, I believe very strongly that developing children's creativity and imagination is one of the most important things we can do for them. School does seem to have a tendency to knock much of the creative, imaginative and adventurous spirit out of us. I suppose I can understand why this has to be – there's simply so much to get done, so many topics to cover, so many skills to learn. But without creativity and imagination, our lives would be soulless; without books, music and art, our world would be very dull indeed.

My subjects do, of course, revolve around the idea of being creative, and perhaps you feel that there is far less need for creativity in your area of the curriculum. But it's not just the disciplines of English, drama, art, music, and so on that require creativity and imagination. Think of some of the great scientific breakthroughs, such as the understanding that the Earth is round and not flat, and the discovery of gravity. In order to propose and prove these 'discoveries', the ability to make an initial imaginative leap was required. For example, gravity is invisible, and it took a creative jump to make the connection between an apple falling to the ground and the possibility of this invisible force.

In this chapter you'll find lots of ideas for developing your children's creativity and imagination. I show you how these thinking skills can be applied and developed right across the curriculum. I look at both written and spoken creativity, at speculation, thinking 'outside the box', lateral thought, and so on. I hope that I can

146

encourage you to take a creative, imaginative approach in your classroom, whatever subject you teach.

Creativity and thought

First and foremost, thinking creatively is all about expressing ourselves in a unique and imaginative way. The word 'creativity' describes the process of bringing something new into being, whether this is a story, a work of art, a scientific discovery, and so on. The human spirit of imagination and invention is harnessed to come up with an original product of some kind. Applying our creativity means being able to take unusual or innovative approaches to the commonplace or ordinary. When we apply our creativity, we might be:

- combining things that we already know, but in an original way;
- seeing something old in a new light;
- taking an unusual approach to solve a problem;
- coming up with an alternative course of action;
- applying lateral thought to take a sideways step in our thinking.

There can be a tendency to view creativity in school as being closely connected to the 'artistic' subjects, such as English, art, drama and music. However, it can just as easily be about applying original thought to create something new in subjects such as science or maths. There is no right or wrong when we're being creative, simply different ways of expressing ourselves.

Creativity is often a fun and exhilarating process for our children, one in which they become excited to witness their own imaginative potential. However, as teachers we should be aware that it can also bring up issues and emotions that are hard to deal with, and consequently we must be sensitive about where the thinking might lead.

Developing creativity

Although some people do seem to find it easier to be creative than others, the level of creativity that each of us has is not fixed. There are plenty of different ways in which we can actually encourage our students to develop their creativity, whatever the subject we are teaching. Here are a number of different thoughts to get you started.

- *Stay open to new ideas:* The successful creative thinker is very much one who remains open to new ideas at all times. When an idea does occur, however bizarre it might appear, the creative thinker welcomes it with open arms. When our children are working on creative tasks, we should take care not to veto or criticize any unusual ideas that they produce. Often, the strangest thoughts will lead to the most imaginative outcomes.
- *Focus on the task at hand:* When applying creativity, our students need to focus very fully on the activity to have the maximum chance of success. Being absorbed in the task helps them to free up the creative elements of their minds. In terms of classroom management, this means that the teacher needs to ensure that the class as a whole demonstrates a high level of concentration. Otherwise, with lots of noise going on, the students will not be able to focus properly on the work. You can find lots of ideas about developing this skill in Chapter 2 of this book.
- *See old things in a new way:* There is very little that is truly 'new' in the world, and often being creative means seeing and responding to commonplace things in a new way, rather than actually coming up with a completely original idea. To encourage your children to see old things in a new way, you might take an ordinary item or task and ask them to come up with some extraordinary ways of approaching it. For example, you could set them an activity in which they must come up with 20 different ways of using a sheet of paper, as opposed to simply writing or drawing on it. The list might include:
  o making a paper aeroplane out of it;
  o using it to make origami animals;
  o colouring and cutting it to make some clothes for a doll;
  o tearing it into tiny pieces to make confetti.
- *Observe closely:* When we are aiming to get our students looking at the commonplace in new ways, it is well worth spending some time on close-up observations. During these observations,

they should be encouraged to respond with all their different senses (see below). For example, you might bring in some pebbles and ask the children to spend five minutes looking closely at them, before talking or writing about what they noticed.

- *Use all the senses:* Encouraging our students to respond to the tasks we set with all their senses will help them develop their creativity. Because we gain so much information from what we see, this sense tends to be quite highly developed. However, learning to use the rest of their senses will give your children a wider basis for their creativity. For example, in the activity suggested above involving pebbles, you might ask the children to close their eyes for a full minute and respond solely with their sense of touch. Holding the pebble in their hands, they could spend the time considering the texture, weight and shape of the object. Sensory information gathered in this way can lead to some highly creative responses.
- *Use intuition:* One excellent way of developing creativity is to encourage our students to find ways of accessing and using their intuition. This is perhaps one of the least used of our abilities, one that most of us tend to ignore in our day-to-day living. Intuition has been called the 'sixth sense' – a sense that goes beyond our immediate and rational responses to the world, and one that normally remains hidden or ignored. Taking an intuitive response means allowing room for our gut feelings and first instincts to come into play, letting impulse rather than logic guide us. Here are a couple of exercises that will help encourage your children to respond intuitively, and also to consider the potential dangers in a solely intuitive reaction.
  o *The (haunted?) house:* Tell the class a story in which a child is walking alone at night, and comes across a strange-looking house. Describe the house, making it sound as spooky and scary as you can. Pause the story at the point when the child first approaches the house, and ask the class to respond intuitively to decide what he or she should do next. Discuss the different gut reactions and spend some time considering how and why the intuition works in this scenario.

149

○ *Who's the villain?* Give the children a list of characters who were present at a large country house when a murder took place. Describe each person's appearance and personality. Now ask the class to decide who the murderer is, relying solely on their first, instinctive response. Again, you could spend some time talking about why particular people were chosen over the others, and whether the villain was chosen on a stereotypical basis.

– *Tap into the subconscious:* Alongside our intuition, if we can learn to tap into our subconscious thoughts, we will often find plenty of material for creative work. In the section on imagination below, you will see two exercises that do just this. When writing a stream of consciousness the rational self is sublimated, in an attempt to hotline directly into the subconscious part of the mind. Similarly, in the forest exercise explained below, the images that each child conjures up will be coming from the subconscious part of the brain. Exploring our dreams and undertaking meditations are two further ways of tapping into our deepest thoughts.

– *Let them play:* As our children progress through school, there is less and less time given over to simply playing. When it comes to creative thinking, playing around is a great way of freeing up our minds and gathering new insights or ideas. When you are aiming to develop creative thinking, it really is worth while giving over some time to letting your students play, whatever their age. This play might take the form of specific games, or it could be simply letting the children play as they wish (perhaps with some clothes and props in a dressing-up area). When we play, the mind is encouraged to experiment, to just let the imagination have a wander around to see what comes up. The absence of pressure and specific goals will often give rise to extremely creative outcomes.

– *Use brainstorming:* Using brainstorms is a wonderful way of coming up with lots of different ideas. Some (perhaps most) of these ideas will be relatively ordinary and uninspired, but others might just be highly creative and original. You can find lots of information about using this format in Chapter 4 of this book.

- *Encourage thinking 'outside the box':* This term refers to a style of thinking in which we move beyond what is considered normal and safe, taking a step outside the 'box' within which we are normally constrained. You can find a whole section below devoted to ways of developing thinking outside the box.

- *Teach lateral thinking:* In a similar way to working outside the box, lateral thinking involves us taking a sideways move from our starting point. When we think laterally we follow connections that lead us into new, and often more creative, territory. Again, this technique is explained in more detail further on in this chapter.

- *Get them inspired!* When trying to develop creativity in our classrooms, it is the teacher's role to inspire his or her children. There are various ways in which this might be done. One way that I have found to be particularly useful for developing creative thought, and in addition for getting the children engaged with the work, is through the use of props. These props are simply objects that are not normally found within the classroom, which the students can use in making creative and original responses.

- *Surprise them!* I love to open my lessons with a surprise – it grips the children and also makes them take a sideways step in their normal thinking and responses to the school day. Getting out of the rut of normal everyday classroom life is a great way of encouraging creativity. For instance, this might mean using unusual openers such as the 'dog food' lesson described in my book *Getting the Buggers to Behave*. It could be turning up at class dressed in historical garb for a lesson on a particular time period. Whatever you choose to do, the teacher who can surprise his or her class will jolt the students into more creative and original thinking.

- *Be a big kid:* Children do often demonstrate the best creativity because they have the least fear of being seen as odd and socially unacceptable. (Of course, this lack of concern is quickly stamped out of them during the process of growing up.) Perhaps one of the best ways of encouraging creative thinking is to give your students the opportunity to be children, no matter whether they are five years old or 15. This means giving them the chance to muck around, to play games, to use imaginative role plays, and so on. In addition to letting your children be children, it also helps a great deal if the teacher is able to act as a big kid as well. This might mean summoning up the courage to chuck out the curriculum once in a while, or simply behaving in a childlike way, retaining that sense of wonder that we all had at one time.

– *Develop a creativity area:* Finally, why not set up a place within your classroom where there are lots of different bits which can be used in whichever way the children want? These 'bits' might be magazines, scissors, stickers, different materials such as beads and coloured string, and so on. This idea is perhaps particularly useful at primary level, where time in a creative area could be built into a rota of different subject-related group work. However, there is no reason at all why it could not also be put into place at secondary level.

The role of imagination

As with all creative approaches, imagination is a very individualized area of thinking. Given the same imaginative task, no two people will come up with the same answers. In fact, where imagination is concerned, there is no such thing as a 'right' or 'wrong' answer, simply a whole host of different approaches and creative outcomes. This means that creative and imaginative work in the classroom is open to all our students, regardless of their academic abilities. In fact it is my experience that some of the least academically able children will let their imaginations run riot when given the chance.

What, then, is imagination? First and foremost it's the ability to think up (and believe in) things that aren't really real. For instance, as we read a book we might conjure up the world it describes inside our heads, using our mind's eye to visualize the action. We might also use our imagination when making up new stories, drawing pictures of strange new worlds, or inventing bizarre new machines. The creation of fantasy seems much easier for children, who have less fear of appearing weird, or being incorrect or failing. Below are ideas for two different activities that you could use in the classroom to develop your children's imaginative thought processes.

The stream of consciousness

This exercise allows the children to 'tip out' their thoughts onto the page, and subsequently to narrow down the focus of their thinking. It allows the imagination to run free, tapping into the deepest roots of our subconscious thinking. The aim of the exercise is to silence the internal editor who normally speaks in our ears when we are writing, and to remove any concerns about the need to write in a technically correct way. By doing this, the imagination is given space to flow freely, without any fear of producing 'bad' writing. This exercise provides an excellent warm-up or starter activity, no matter what the topic of the actual lesson. It gets the children's writing flowing freely, and also helps them focus their thoughts into the classroom. Here's how the exercise works.

- Explain to the class that when you say 'go', they are to begin writing and not to pause until you say 'stop'.
- They can write whatever they wish, the idea being to keep writing whatever pops into their heads.
- Tell them that if they get stuck, they should simply keep writing the same word over and over again, until they get unstuck.
- The aim is to keep the pen flowing at all times, writing as quickly as possible, so as to capture the imaginative thoughts without any interference.
- Let the children know that they do not need to worry about punctuation or spelling.
- After about two or three minutes, stop the class and ask the children to count how many words they have written.
- They should divide this number in half: for instance, if they wrote 50 words, this would be halved to make 25. If they have an odd number, this should be divided to the nearest whole number, so 63 would become either 31 or 32.
- Give them a short time (about five minutes) to cut the number of words on the page down into exactly half the amount which they started with, crossing out the words they do not want.

- It is up to them how they go about editing, perhaps choosing to keep words that seem particularly important or interesting.
- Once they have cut the number in half, repeat the process, asking them to divide the remaining amount in half again so that they end up with a quarter of the original total.
- They should then spend some time putting these words into a different order, to create an interesting 'word picture'.
- You might like to ask for some volunteers to read their word pictures out to the class.
- You can adapt this exercise by giving a 'starter word' on which the class will write, for instance, 'blue', 'morning', 'rainstorm', and so on.

A journey into the imagination

Journeys provide us with a wonderful metaphor for the process of education. For instance, every lesson that we teach is a journey in which we lead our children through a number of activities until they arrive at their destination. In a good lesson, the destination will be a place where they understand something new, where they have learned about a new subject, or perhaps acquired new skills. When we're aiming to develop our students' thinking skills, taking a journey into the imagination is a fantastic way to show them the power of their own creativity. As the children go inside their heads, and follow their thoughts wherever they lead, they will start to understand how individual and original each person's imagination can be.

The focus exercises in Chapter 2 offer an excellent way of developing your children's focus and concentration in short bursts. The 'Into the forest' exercise described below offers you the chance for a more lengthy period of imaginative focus. It is particularly useful for either the start or the end of lessons, as it is an excellent way of getting your students into the right frame of mind for work, or of calming them down (perhaps after a particularly active lesson).

First get the children sitting comfortably (they can lie down if you have the space), and ask them to close their eyes. You then take them 'into the forest', talking them through the experience in a general way, posing questions that allow for individual decisions, and letting your students fill in the blanks. Here are some tips about how best to do this exercise.

- *Encourage the use of the senses:* As you talk to the class on their way through the forest, make sure that you ask them questions that encourage them to use all their senses. Talk to them about what they can see, hear, smell, touch and even taste, as applicable. Not only will this make the whole experience much more vivid, but it will also help them develop their imaginative powers.
- *Offer some alternatives:* Although your aim is for the children to create their own imaginative worlds, it is useful to offer some possible experiences for those who might find the exercise difficult at first. For instance, in the example below you'll see that I say *'Now you start to walk down a path. Perhaps the bushes have thorns that catch at your legs, or perhaps the path is wide and easy to walk down.'* By making suggestions in this way you can light the spark that will ignite the children's imaginative thought processes.
- *Use a hypnotic tone of voice:* Tone of voice is very important in teaching, and perhaps nowhere more so than when we are trying to fire our children's imaginations. As you describe the journey through the forest, try to use a hypnotic tone of voice to create a calm and relaxing atmosphere. This will ensure that your children gain full benefit from their imaginative journey.
- *Take your time:* With all the time pressures of the classroom, it is very tempting to rush through the exercise to 'get it finished'. However, this activity will be far more valuable if you spend a good amount of time on it. Talk slowly, leaving gaps when you ask a question, so that the children have time to consider what you have said. Allow them the space to build a vivid picture inside their heads.
- *'Wing it':* Rather than planning ahead of time exactly what you're going to say, it can be a good idea to simply 'wing it', making the journey up as you go along. This allows space for the teacher's own imagination to come into play.
- *Explore the individual responses:* When you have finished the exercise, it is well worth spending some time discussing the

experiences of individual children. You will find lots of willing volunteers who are very keen to describe what they saw, heard, felt, and so on. You will also be amazed at the huge variety of different forests, buildings and figures.

- *Make some interpretations:* Psychoanalysts might say that our responses to this exercise can be subjected to interpretation. For instance, some believe that the building represents our ambition, the person or figure what stands in our way, etc. Why not talk with your class about how their individual journeys could be interpreted? By doing this, you will help them to use metacognition, the process whereby we explore the way in which our own minds and thoughts actually work (thinking about how we think).

- *Take them to different places:* Once you've done the initial exercise, try to think up lots of different settings into which you can lead your children. The only limit to this exercise is your imagination! (In fact, why not ask your class for some additional suggestions for where you might travel next?) Here are three examples to get you started:
  o a hot and dusty desert;
  o the snowy wastes of Antarctica;
  o an alien planet.

To give you a better idea of how the exercise works, here is an example of what you might say as you take your class 'into the forest'. This opening section sets the scene, and it's then down to the individual teacher to decide what happens next.

You're standing in a forest, in a clearing. Look around – what can you see? What noises can you hear? What type of trees are surrounding you? Is it a damp, tropical rainforest, or is it a forest in this country? What is the weather like? Is it day or night? Are there wild animals in the trees, or are you completely alone, with just the song of birds to accompany you? Now you start to walk down a path. Perhaps the bushes have thorns that catch at your legs, or perhaps the path is wide and easy to walk down. As you walk, take the time to look around you at the forest. After a few minutes, you see a building in the distance. What sort of building do you see? Is it a tall stone tower, or perhaps a falling-down wooden hut? You head towards the building and arrive at the door. Stretch out your hand to touch the door – how does it feel? Is it rough or smooth? What does the handle look like? You open the door slowly and step inside, looking around at this strange new place. Can you see furniture in the room, or is it empty? Suddenly you notice a figure in the room. Who is it? Is it a person or an animal? Or is it something else . . .

Thinking 'outside the box'

When we're aiming to develop our children's creativity, it is abso-lutely vital that we encourage them to think 'outside the box'. This phrase provides a very useful metaphor for the process whereby we step outside and beyond the 'box' that we normally inhabit. Our aim is to help our children develop the risky, intui-tive, oblique parts of their thinking processes, rather than always sticking with the more logical, rational and linear ways of working. Normal thinking is often constrained by the fear of failure, whereas when we think outside the box we allow our-selves to think unusual, strange, abnormal thoughts, without any internal or external censorship. The mind's urge to place order and structures on what it thinks must be is put to one side for a little while.

Thinking outside the box allows us to play around with differ-ent ideas and ways of doing things. It does require us to be willing to take risks with our thinking, as well as to be playful with the ideas that we have. For this reason, it may take a while before your students are brave enough to take their thoughts in these directions, although in fact you may find them much more open to this type of thinking than adults would be in a similar situation. Here are some thoughts about how you can encourage your stu-dents to think in a playful way, moving outside the box with their ideas.

- *What would happen if . . .?* Get your children posing the ques-tion *'What would happen if . . .?'*, making the 'if' a strange or completely off the wall idea. For instance, you might ask *'What would happen if cars ran on sea water?'* This initial stimulus will encourage your children to extend their thinking in unusual directions, moving outside the box of normal thought. So they might come up with a description of a world in which people pull up at a beach to refuel their vehicles, and in which the sea replaces oil as a valuable commodity, causing fights to break out between countries over who owns the coastline.

- *Making wild and crazy suggestions:* Many of the most creative breakthroughs in human endeavour must have seemed completely crazy at first. Before the flight of the first spaceship, it would have seemed completely insane to suggest that one day human beings would be landing on the moon. When solving a problem, or approaching other areas of thinking, ask your students to come up with 'crazy' suggestions as well as the more obvious ideas that first occur to them. The section further on in this chapter entitled 'Creativity and thinking ahead' gives you some more thoughts on this area.

- *Finding many answers to one question:* As we saw in the section on open and closed questioning, asking a closed question tends to have the effect of stifling the potential for more complex thought. When we're aiming to be creative, and to think outside the box, our goal should be to find as many answers to any single question as is possible. Again, the more unusual suggestions will often lead to greater creativity.

- *Doodling and drawing:* When we're aiming to think outside the box, we need to tap into the kind of subconscious and intuitive thoughts discussed in the section on 'Developing creativity'. By using these areas of our minds, we tend to access more original ideas. One way of doing this is to use doodling and drawing. By circumventing the use of language in response to a task and instead allowing our hands to wander on the page, we can encourage the creative subconscious to come out.

- *Daydreaming:* In our dreams, we sometimes stumble across answers to problems that have been puzzling us for a long time. When we are asleep the rational part of the mind is sublimated, and the subconscious takes over. Obviously we cannot make our children dream at school, but what we can do is to get them daydreaming instead.

- *Making mistakes:* It is only through a process of making mistakes, and learning from them, that we are able to master skills and grasp concepts. Babies are not born able to walk, but by about one year of age they have become toddlers. Along the way, the baby has to make many mistakes, at first only being able to crawl, and eventually walking but falling over. The same applies when it comes to encouraging creative thinking in our classrooms. If we can persuade our students not to be afraid to sound silly or odd, we will open up the possibility for eventual success. Sometimes mistakes will lead us to a creative solution that a search for what is 'correct' would have failed to find.

- *Using the unexpected:* I'm a great fan of the unexpected in teaching. Our children come to their lessons expecting normality, and when they are faced with something odd, weird or startling, this forces them to make a sudden adjustment in their perspective. By changing their mindset in this way, we can inspire them to think 'outside the box'. This might mean using strange stimuli, for instance bringing in an engaging prop, or starting a lesson with a theatrical 'bang' of some type (whether metaphorical or literal!). It might also mean changing the seating arrangements around so that the children are forced to see the classroom and the lesson from a fresh point of view.

Lateral thinking

Just as with thinking outside the box, lateral thinking is about moving beyond what is immediately obvious. When we think laterally, we aim to make sideways connections, jumping away from our original starting point. In order to do this, we need to go beyond the mindset whereby we see thought as linear process, with one thought following another in a logical sequence. Often, when we approach a thinking task in this linear way, we end up in a cul-de-sac in which we cannot see how we might move onwards. By taking a sideways jump, we can come up with new ideas, look at a problem, task or other scenario in a different way, or face an issue with a fresh perspective.

For instance, in writing the original edition of this book, I faced a big problem when it came to writing the final section. I spent ages bogged down in my thinking, in the metaphorical cul-de-sac described above, unable to see how I could solve the problem that I faced. Eventually, though, I managed to take a lateral thought jump whereby I came upon the answer. Often, these leaps in thinking will come about without a conscious effort, as happened for me with my final-chapter problem.

However, although my solution was based on a 'eureka moment' in which I suddenly saw where the answer lay, there was, of course, a series of thoughts involved. Here's a description of the (torturous) thinking processes that I undertook to come to my final decision, including the points at which I used lateral thinking to its full advantage. You'll find the promised new chapter, together with readers' contributions, at the end of this second edition of the book.

- I don't like what I've written – it just doesn't seem to work.
- The problem is, I don't know enough about other subjects to write about thinking in them.
- Should I cut this chapter?
- No, I want to keep it, I'm really interested in thinking across the curriculum, and I believe that teachers would want to read about it.
- How can I find the information I need to include here?
- I could spend ages researching different curriculum areas, but there's just too much to cover.
- In any case, even if I have the relevant information, I don't feel that I can assess what is useful or relevant unless I'm an expert in a particular subject.
- *Lateral jump – away from the fixed idea that I personally have to write this chapter on my own.*
- Who would know enough about the different subjects?
- I could approach a school and ask teachers from different curriculum areas to contribute their ideas. (I was in fact hoping to do this, but the idea didn't come to fruition.)
- *Lateral jump – away from the need to 'do it now'.*
- What about involving my readers? They will be from all different subject areas.

160

- Why don't I pose the final chapter as an invitation to contribute their ideas, and include these in the second edition?
- Let's go for it – I'll junk what I've already written and use this approach instead. I feel that it fits in perfectly with the whole style and tone of my books.

Creativity and thinking ahead

As I mentioned in the opening to this chapter, some of the great scientific breakthroughs have come about as a result of intellectual leaps that involved creative thought. So it is that, as Newton sat under his apple tree and winced when the apple hit him on the head, he had to take a creative approach to come up with the idea of gravity. He could not actually see this force but he had to be able to think in an imaginative way, speculating that it might exist in order to explain how it works.

If you're an avid reader of science fiction, or if you enjoy television programmes such as *Star Trek*, then you might have noticed how many of the ideas in science fiction eventually become reality. In his book *1984*, George Orwell foresees a 'Big Brother' watching over us, keeping track of our movements. Not only has this term come into common usage via a recent television programme, but inventions such as CCTV mean that we are actually being watched. Similarly, the communicators that the crew use on *Star Trek* are eerily reminiscent of the mobile phones that we so take for granted today.

Herein lies one of the wonderful and fascinating points about creativity – much of that which at first seems far too bizarre or strange to work is eventually assimilated into our way of life, becoming a normal part of everyday living. So catching an aeroplane flight is now something that many people have done, whereas little more than a century ago this would have seemed completely impossible and totally crazy.

When you're aiming to develop creativity, why not encourage your children to experiment with thinking ahead? For instance, you could set them a task that asks them to imagine what the world will be like at some future date. They might think about areas such as:

- what sort of jobs we will do;
- what type of houses we will live in;
- how the environment might have changed;
- what new inventions would have been created;
- how we will travel;
- where we will take our holidays;
- what school might be like (and whether it will even exist!).

Speculation

The thesaurus on my computer gives a number of interesting alternatives for the word 'speculation'. These include 'conjecture', 'rumour', 'assumption', 'theory' and 'guesswork'. Speculation is, to my mind, the creative twin sister of hypothesis. Whereas hypothesizing suggests a more structured, factually based and logical approach, speculation is a little looser and rather more creative. When we speculate, we allow our brains to view known information in an imaginative, original way. This creative aspect of speculation means that it can offer some wonderful and inspirational starting points for work in our classrooms. You'll see from the answers to the exercise below just where wild speculation might take you!

- Pose the following question to your class: *'A close friend has been acting very strangely. In the past month she has bought a new car, a new house, and a whole new set of clothes. What could have happened?'*
- Now ask the students to speculate about the answer to this question, coming up with at least five different possibilities.
- Use these answers to spark off some writing or speaking work, for instance, creating stories or short dramas about the scenario.
- Here are some possible answers, ranging from the probable to the totally incredible. As you'll see, each one would provide excellent material for a story or other imaginative activities.

o She's won the lottery but doesn't want anyone to know.
o She was involved in a bank robbery and is spending the proceeds.
o She has discovered a way to turn base metal into gold.
o She's been taken up to a spacecraft from another planet and replaced by an alien, who has come to take over the world.

Speculation is excellent for developing creativity in all areas of the curriculum. You might use some 'What would happen if . . .?' questions as described in the section on 'Thinking outside the box', and relate them to your own subject. In science this might mean asking *'What would happen if computers could run on solar power?'* In maths you could pose the question *'What would happen if we only had the numbers 1 to 5?'*

Language and creativity

Language is a wonderfully creative medium in which to work, and also an excellent tool for developing the imagination. Whatever subject you teach, you will be using language to communicate with your students, and they with you. Whether we are simply using language to talk about an idea, or applying it in a more focused way, as in the examples that follow, it is a very useful tool for developing our students' creativity. Below, you'll find some ideas and exercises that you can use in your classroom which combine language and creative thinking.

Symbolism: and metaphor and smile

Understanding and using the concept of symbolism (and its close relatives metaphor and simile) require the use of higher-order thinking. A symbol is a way of linking two similar ideas together to develop or deepen a description. For instance, you might use the image *'as cool as a cucumber'* to describe a character who is very calm and composed. Using the idea of a cucumber helps us imagine the person, and his or her attitude, more fully. Similes use two different formats: either *'as x as an x'* or *'x is like x'*. An example of the second format would be: *'The sun is like a yellow balloon'*.

Here's an exercise that you can use with your students to develop their creativity, and to get them working with and using language at its fullest. The class are given a 'starter simile', in which they have only the first part of the image. They must then come up with as many different and creative ideas as possible for completing the phrase. You might like to give a prize for either the most examples found, or alternatively the most creative idea suggested. Here are some ideas to get you started:

- 'As hot as . . .'
  o 'the sun'
  o 'a bonfire on a summer's day'
  o 'George Clooney'
- 'As big as . . .'
  o 'a house'
  o 'a pregnant elephant'
  o 'a sumo wrestler's pants'

Dingbats

This popular word game makes use of the double meanings inherent in language. It asks the players to turn words into a picture to pose a puzzle – and vice versa to work out what is meant. The images used are very literal, and the ability to find the meaning requires the player to be able to 'read' them as they would be said. The students must think creatively to come up with ideas for their pictures, and also use lateral thought to come to their solutions. The game works as follows:

- Divide your class up into groups, and either give each group a saying to work on, or ask them to come up with a suggestion of their own. You can see some sample phrases below. (Alternatively, you could ask the children to work individually.)
- The children must describe this phrase using only a picture. The picture should provide a literal representation of the saying that can be worked out by 'reading' the image.

- The individuals or groups then come to the front of the classroom and either hold up their pictures, or draw them on the board.
- The rest of the class must work out what the saying is. You might give points to those children or groups who answer correctly.

The examples below will help you to get started. For the first phrase I've included some comments on the thought processes involved, to show you how the children must think laterally to understand the picture.

'Too hot to handle.' A picture of a '2' in flames, followed by another '2' making up a handle on a door.

Thought processes:

- The number '2' is a homophone. It might also represent the words 'too' or 'to'.
- The burning '2' would be hot, because of the flames.
- The second '2' looks like the handle on a door, and could therefore mean '2 handle'. Again, using the homophone, this could be turned into 'to handle'.

'Cup of tea.' A cup containing an oversized letter 'T'.

'Paint the town red.' A group of buildings half-painted red. Alongside a bucket of red paint with a paintbrush.

'Up to no good.' An arrow pointing upwards to the words 'no good'.

Invented words

In the poem 'Jabberwocky' by Lewis Carroll, the poet uses a mixture of real and invented words to tell his story. You can use the idea of an invented language to develop your children's thinking skills, particularly in the area of creativity. Coming up with new words that actually make some sort of sense, at the same time as being purely imaginary, is not easy at all. Here's the first verse of 'Jabberwocky' so you can see how Carroll does it.

'Twas brillig, and the slithy toves
Did gyre and gimble in the wabe:
All mimsy were the borogroves,
And the mome raths outgrabe.

Now here's a quick outline of how you might use this poem within your classroom.

- Read the poem through, and discuss what is going on. Ask your children to think about how it is still possible to 'understand' what is said, despite the fact that many of the words do not exist in the English language.
- Spend some time trying to find words in English that might match up with the new words that Carroll uses. Encourage your students to be creative and wide-ranging in their responses, rather than trying to decide on what would be 'correct'.
- Once the children have explored the poem in this way they can then move on to develop their own invented words and languages.
- You might give them a list of words that they must 'translate' and then discuss what they come up with.
- Alternatively, you could ask them to write a creative piece of some sort, such as a poem or story, in which some of the invented words are used.
- Another idea is to get the students writing scripts of a conversation in their invented language, and then perhaps performing these to the class.

The idea above would be applicable to an English lesson at primary or secondary level. However, there are plenty of ways of using invented words within other subjects to develop creative thought and also to have some fun. As well as encouraging creativity, this exercise also requires the children to think about how the words that we use are related to what they describe. When they make up their own vocabulary, this must be given an appropriate sound, and relate sensibly to the context in which it will be used. Here are a few ideas about using invented words across the curriculum to give you some inspiration.

- In a religious education lesson, ask the students to invent a new religion. Ask them to come up with equivalent terms for points such as:
  o the name of the religion;
  o the name of the God or gods;
  o a place of worship (for example, temple, church);
  o artefacts that are used during services;
  o names for different pieces of clothing related to the religion.
- In a maths lesson, ask the class to come up with some invented terms for different shapes, or alternatively for commands such as 'add', 'subtract', or 'multiply'.
- In a geography lesson, ask the children to devise alternative names for features on a map. To spice this exercise up, you might tell them that an alien map has been discovered, in which the aliens give new names to the different parts of the Earth's landscape.

Perhaps one of the most fascinating examples of an invented language is provided by the slang that our students use outside the classroom (and often inside it as well). There is plenty of scope for studying and developing creativity here. For instance, you might spend some time discussing the different slang terms that your children know of, and how these might have been created. You could then move on to getting them to invent further slang words of their own, and having 'secret' conversations in this new 'language'. Just one word of warning – a lot of slang terms have what you might deem to be inappropriate content, so you will need to discuss the handling of this with your class before you start.

Images and creativity

Images offer us a great way into developing creative thinking skills, and particularly into looking at the area of interpretation.

If a number of different people examine the same picture, they will each see and think about something different. One person might focus on the use of light and dark or on different colours, while another notices the characters in the image and immediately tries to construct a storyline about them. Of course, pictures have great potential when it comes to sparking off imaginative and creative work. They also play an important part in allowing our children to respond with something more than language. Here are some thoughts about the different types of pictures you might use to develop thinking in your classroom, right across the curriculum.

- *Postcards:* The teacher could collect, or ask the students to bring in, postcards from different places around the world. This could lead the class on to discussing what it might be like to live in these countries, applying creative thinking to form an image of a very different place.
- *Photographs:* There is something very captivating about photographs. Not only do they show us a frozen image from real life, but they also give us a snapshot of a specific moment in time. You might decide to ask your children to bring in photographs on a particular topic, such as 'family life'. Alternatively, you could obtain some copies of photographs from the past, or of great moments in history. An excellent question to get the thinking started could be: *'Does the camera ever lie?'*
- *Works of art:* Great pieces of art provide you with an engaging starting point for creative thinking work. You might talk about the notion of art with your class, and why certain paintings and sculptures are considered 'great'. Alternatively, you could look at technique: how a work is structured and painted, what the emotion or inspiration for the picture was, how colour, shadow and light are used, and so on. You might also take some time to think about the meanings within a picture, and whether there are any metaphors, messages, or other allusions.
- *Symbolism:* Pictures can have great symbolic content, just as texts can when we are examining language. By looking into the layers of meaning within a picture, we encourage our children

to make connections, and also to develop their higher-order thinking.

Discussion questions

The following questions will help you stimulate discussion when the students are looking at and thinking about different pictures. They will help you explore how creativity works, and also give you some imaginative starting points for further activities.

- *'Where is this?'*
- *'What is happening in the picture?'*
- *'What might have happened just before this moment?'*
- *'What could happen just after this moment?'*
- *'Which characters can you see in the picture?'*
- *'Is there anyone or anything else just outside the picture?'*
- *'Can you see any buildings or other constructions?'*
- *'What type of people might live in these buildings?'*
- *'What objects can you see in the picture?'*
- *'Could these objects have any double meanings? If so, what do you think these meanings are?'*
- *'What colours are used in the picture?'*
- *'How do the colours add to the mood or emotions in the picture?'*
- *'Are there any hidden messages in the picture? What are these messages and how are they put across?'*

These questions have the potential to lead on to a whole range of different discussion points for developing your children's thinking. For instance, the question *'Which characters can you see in the picture?'* might lead on to questions about what these characters are thinking or feeling, the type of jobs they do, the status that they have relative to each other, and so on.

Into the picture

The exercise described below gives you one idea for working with pictures in your classroom, when aiming to develop creative thinking and imaginative responses.

169

- Find postcards that show a number of different settings. Then either ask the children to pick an image which interests them, or alternatively just give out the postcards on a random basis.
- Ask the students to close their eyes and imagine they are a person just walking into the place in the picture. Tell them to look around and really take in all that this setting has to offer. They might consider what they can see, hear, smell, taste or feel; they could imagine what the weather feels like, and so on. Ask them to look all around, turning to the right and left, and also looking behind themselves.
- Next, tell your students to turn right and walk. Pose some questions to encourage their imagination, for instance:
  o *'Where are you going?'*
  o *'What else can you see as you walk?'*
  o *'Are there any other people or animals here?'*
  o *'What are they doing?'*
- Once you have finished walking your students through the picture, you might ask them to use what they imagined as a basis for some creative writing.

8

Thinking and ideas

This chapter deals with finding, and working with, different ideas. The ideas that I cover fall into two different categories: creative ideas, such as devising new inventions or making up storylines, and the personal beliefs and ideas that we hold about the 'big' questions of life. In the classroom, you might be exploring new ways of recycling waste within a science lesson. Alternatively, you could be studying the ideas contained within PSHE topics, such as drugs or bullying, which require the children to come up with viewpoints and opinions of their own. Beyond the classroom, our children will be working out their own ideas about what their lives are actually all about – their personal philosophies of life and death. For some this will mean taking on the religious beliefs of their parents and community; for others it might involve questioning the tenets of traditional faiths.

Many of the ideas that I examine in this chapter involve a very personal way of thinking. This applies particularly to those ideas involved with looking for meaning in our lives. Although both rational and creative thought might be used in approaching these questions, essentially the view that our students take will be subjective and private. This does mean that the teacher needs to approach these areas of thinking with great care and sensitivity, as well as with a good dose of open-mindedness. It is all too easy for us to project our own values and feelings onto what we teach, particularly when it comes to issues of personal belief. We must struggle hard to resist this temptation, allowing our children to establish their own personal thoughts about what is 'true'.

You'll find a whole host of strategies and exercises in this chapter to help you develop your children's thinking about ideas. I look at how you can help your children in finding new or interesting ideas of their own. I also explore the issue of consequences, in which we examine where our actions might lead. You'll find a section on the weighty issue of morality and religious ideas. I also look at some unusual ways of structuring work on ideas in the classroom.

Some thoughts about ideas

Ideas really are a wonderful example of exactly what our brains can do when we start thinking. Without the ability to come up with new ideas, the human race would still be living in caves, hunting mammoth for dinner and grunting loudly to communicate. We all come up with ideas practically every single minute of every day, or pose ourselves internal questions asking what we believe about the world. This might be as basic as *'Have you got any ideas about what we can have for dinner?'* It could be as complex and potentially important as a scientist saying *'I've got an idea about a new treatment for diabetes.'* It might be as fundamentally life changing as asking ourselves *'What do I believe will happen to me after I die, and how will this affect the way in which I live?'*

Ideas come in many shapes and forms, and they lend themselves to work in all areas of the school curriculum. They are closely linked to the imaginative and creative side of our personalities, as they require us to be original and innovative. They are also tied to the more logical side of our brains, for instance, when following a series of ideas in a logical train of thought to see where the truth might lie. In fact, when finding and working with ideas we have the opportunity to link both the creative and the logical sides of our brains. For instance, we might be creative in our search for new ways to power an engine, whilst simultaneously using logic to answer the question *'How else can we make a vehicle move?'* Once we have come up with an idea, we need to test whether it will work, and this requires the application of logic and reasoning.

The 'big' ideas that I explore in this chapter involve a more personal and subjective approach to our thinking. When it comes to looking at the beliefs that people hold, the thinking involves neither a fully rational nor a purely creative approach. Instead, it is about deciding what we as individuals actually believe – those ideas that we personally hold to be true and valid. Here are just a few of the myriad ways in which ideas have helped make us what we are.

- *Inventions:* From the wheel to the car, the abacus to the computer, the aeroplane to the spaceship, ideas for new inventions have shaped our world. These new discoveries have made our lives fuller and easier.
- *Scientific theories:* Science has helped us find new ways of looking at and understanding our environment. What we know about our world is not fixed in stone, and so far we have only scratched the surface of discovering how the Earth, and the universe beyond, really works. There is plenty of room for more ideas, so get your students thinking!
- *Creative works:* Artists of all types have given us wonderful material that enriches our lives and makes us think. From the classic works of literature to great pieces of art, from inspirational poetry to music and songs: the ideas behind creative works have a resonance that echoes through our lives.
- *Religion:* From the very earliest times, humans have turned to religion to offer them a way of making sense of the world. The ideas that form religious beliefs are, for some of us, an absolutely vital part of our lives.

Why do we need ideas?

As I pointed out above, without ideas the human race would not have progressed in the way that it has. Ideas play a crucial role in the survival of the human species, and in helping us prosper and develop. We need ideas for a whole range of reasons, including the following:

- *To adapt and survive:* Life on Earth has developed so that certain species thrive, while others die out. Those species that are able to evolve, adapting to suit a changing environment, are most likely to survive. The ability of the human race to come up with new ideas, to find new ways of understanding and interacting with the world, has enabled us to adapt, survive and prosper. To give just one example, the development of irrigation techniques has meant that we can grow food in conditions where this would normally not be possible.
- *Finding better and easier ways to do things:* New inventions have allowed us to find both more efficient and simpler ways of doing a whole variety of tasks. From throwing your dirty clothes into the washing machine to typing and saving text on a computer, human inventions have made our lives more straightforward, leaving us time to stretch ourselves in new directions.
- *Creating works of art:* Art is the expression of the human soul: it entertains and inspires us. Without the ideas that are the basis of all works of art, life would be very dull and colourless.
- *Coming to a sense of self:* We need ideas to help us establish what we believe in and to examine why we believe it. The ideas we have about the big questions of life help us in coming to a sense of ourselves. They also help us change and adapt the way we live our lives in view of our beliefs, making us 'better' people.
- *Dealing with our emotions:* The unanswerable questions of life can cause us fear and anxiety. Children particularly need to come to terms with their fears about issues such as dying and the supernatural. The ideas that the human race has devised, including religious beliefs, help us come to terms with our emotions.

Finding ideas

The ability to find new ideas is an essential part of thought, whether this is coming up with new thoughts through creative thinking, or exploring our personal beliefs and values. Finding ideas is particularly important in the classroom, where it offers the seeds from which learning will grow. Here are some thoughts about how you can encourage your children to find ideas for themselves.

- *Words:* Language is absolutely stuffed with ideas: words can have so many different meanings and connotations, and can help us make a whole variety of connections and associations. You might be brainstorming from a single word to start you off finding ideas on a specific topic. Or you might be practising free association as described in Chapter 4. A single word can start a whole chain of new thoughts and ideas – for example, taking a word such as 'rainbow' and seeing where it leads the class.
- *Doodles:* Ideas do not always have to come about in the form of language. You might encourage your children to doodle, and then examine the shapes and images that they have created, searching for the possibility of new ideas to inspire the class.
- *Trial and error:* Sometimes, a process of trial and error can kick up some fascinating ideas. The random nature of just 'trying things out' can lead to some very interesting results. For instance, a scientist might mix different chemicals together to see what happens; a mathematician could experiment with different formulae in the search for a solution to a number puzzle.
- *Letting the ideas take you for a walk:* Along similar lines, an excellent way of working with some ideas that are only in their infancy is simply to follow them and see where they lead. For example, a writer might have an idea for a character, but no inkling as to the actual storyline. Instead of trying to come up with ideas for the story, the writer could instead simply let the character loose on the page, to see where he or she goes.
- *All around us:* Ideas are all around us, everywhere we look. For instance, the school environment offers us some wonderful opportunities for finding new ideas, if we can open ourselves up to inspiration. A bare patch of earth in the playground might inspire you to start your children working on a nature area. They could come up with ideas for setting it up, putting their thoughts into practice and making a real difference to their environment.

Argument, persuasion and bias

When we employ argument, we are trying to get others to believe in the same ideas as we do. We put forward a case to try to persuade people to see the world as we see it, to understand the opinions that we hold or the position we are coming from. Sometimes, our students will need to make their argument in as rational and objective a way as possible. For instance, if they are developing a line of reasoning about their views on a set text or an historical situation they will need to take a rational and considered approach to their thinking. In these instances, they must fight hard against the temptation to make sweeping generalizations, or to employ emotive language, persuasion and bias.

However, in some contexts and for some tasks it will be entirely justified for our students to use more persuasive, less rational techniques. On some occasions, the beliefs that we hold about a particular issue will form an integral part of the argument that we make and the standpoint that we take. For example, if our children were arguing a firmly held view during a debate about genetic engineering or fox hunting, they would be right to include points that they feel to be justified and 'true', even though others might not necessarily agree with them.

Some ideas and opinions are strongly held, and come fortified by a passionate belief. We can use this passion to start some really strong arguments in our classrooms, for instance by using debates (discussed in the section below). An interesting approach is to ask our students to argue from a standpoint that is diametrically opposed to that which they actually believe. By doing this, we force them to consider other viewpoints, and to push their thinking skills to the limit in finding ways to support their arguments.

Below you'll find some ideas about developing objective arguments and also about using persuasive techniques and spotting bias and manipulation. I also describe an in-role exercise that will help you encourage your students to develop and support their arguments, as well as understanding when bias or persuasion is being used.

Developing an argument

Our aim when developing an argument is to put a series of ideas together in a line of reasoning, and to support the ideas that we propose with the relevant evidence. We will usually come to a conclusion, when we have finished putting our case, which takes into account all the ideas that we have proposed. You can find lots more ideas about developing rational arguments in the section on reasoning in Chapter 6. Here are some points that you can raise with your students when teaching them the thinking behind the development of arguments.

- *Maintain objectivity:* As we discussed above, it is important to keep the argument objective as far as possible. This is actually harder than it sounds, depending on the subject under discussion. If the argument has been written down, for instance in an essay, it's a good idea to check back through the work when it is finished to ensure that the points made are as objective as they can be. The following questions will help your students get started on establishing whether or not they have been objective:
  o Is there any emotion involved in my argument?
  o Do I state any points as facts, when they are actually opinions?
  o Have I left out any points because I could not make them fit my argument?
- *Support each statement:* For every statement that is made, support must be given. This means finding appropriate evidence to back up the ideas that are proposed. Depending on the subject, this evidence might take the form of quotations, factual information, examples from expert sources, and so on.
- *Develop the ideas:* The most successful arguments will include further development of the ideas being proposed. This process requires the application of higher-order thinking, and it is often the area of argument with which our students find most difficulty.
- *Ensure clarity and precision:* It can be tempting for our students to 'over-egg' their argument puddings by using 'floury' language

or lengthy sentences, in the belief that this will gain them better marks. In fact, the best arguments are often those that use the simplest, clearest language with which to propose the ideas. It is the precision of what is said, rather than how 'clever' it sounds, which is important.

- *Consider all views:* As I said above, objectivity is important in creating rational arguments. One way of ensuring this is to consider all potential viewpoints when developing a line of reasoning. You might ask your students to experiment with writing their arguments from several different stances, to see what different people might say on the same subject.

- *Give it some spice:* Although I have emphasized the importance of objectivity and the avoidance of bias, there is no reason why our students should not scatter some persuasive linguistic techniques within what they say. This will help 'spice up' the argument, making it more interesting to read, and more gripping and persuasive to the reader.

Bias and persuasion

Moving on from the completely rational, objective argument, there will be occasions when we need or want to include some persuasive and even biased content in our arguments. This applies particularly when we are developing an argument about an issue, especially when it is one on which people have a variety of viewpoints and opinions. There are various techniques that we might employ to make our argument more persuasive. These include:

- emotive and heartfelt language;
- biased or inaccurate reporting of 'the facts';
- a heavy slant towards one viewpoint;
- over-exaggeration of the information given or points made;
- neglecting to include details that do not fit in with our argument;
- sweeping generalizations that are not backed up by the facts.

Of course, not all of these techniques are entirely fair on the reader or listener, especially when they are not aware that an attempt is being made to influence them. In combination with understanding how they can employ persuasion, our students also need to learn how to spot when they themselves are being manipulated. This is a skill that can be learnt, and it is important that we train our children in how to recognize when bias is being used. This will help them in writing their own argumentative pieces (whether objective or not), and also in seeing when other people are trying to control their thoughts.

You can find some useful examples of persuasive and manipulative techniques, and the use of bias, in tabloid news stories. You might like to use a comparison of different reports of the same story to develop your children's thinking on this issue. Ask them to look through the text and to use a highlighter to pick out words and phrases that are not entirely objective and rational. Here are some questions to use with your class when thinking about whether an argument or set of ideas is fairly put or not.

- *'Is the writer taking a particular stance or viewpoint on the issue?'*
- *'Is the writer entirely objective, or does subjectivity play a part?'*
- *'Is the writer trying to persuade us of a certain point of view?'*
- *'Does the piece contain fact, opinion, or a mixture of the two?'*
- *'Are there any hidden agendas here? If yes, what are they?'*
- *'Are emotive words and phrases used to try and persuade you to a specific viewpoint?'*
- *'Are any of the points made exaggerated or over-emphasized?'*
- *'Are there any factual inaccuracies in the piece?'*
- *'Are these inaccuracies intentional, and designed to persuade you or manipulate you?'*

In-role exercise: the council meeting

Drama provides an excellent structure for thinking about and putting forward ideas, and making and developing arguments. Asking the children to work in role, as in the role-of-the-expert activity described in Chapter 3, is a very powerful motivational and engaging approach. When working in role, your children do not necessarily have to be experts; instead they can play a whole host of different characters. By playing someone else, the students are forced to look at the ideas that many different people might hold. The exercise below will help the children develop a number of different thinking skills. These include:

- using creative thinking to come up with new ideas;
- considering their own viewpoint on the issue being raised;
- using, recognizing and overcoming manipulation and bias;
- justifying statements by offering valid reasons;
- coming to conclusions based on the evidence and opinions given.

Here is how the exercise works:

- The teacher presents a potentially controversial scenario to the class. For instance: *'The school is planning to sell off part of the sports field so that a local supermarket can increase the size of its car park.'*
- To help you engage the class, present the scenario to the class by bringing in a prop. In this example you show them a letter, supposedly from the head teacher to parents, detailing the proposal and how the school will benefit. (These benefits could include a substantial amount of money being given to the school, for instance to spend on a new science block.)
- Ask one of the children to read the letter out, and spend some time in a discussion to explore the initial reactions of the class.
- A council meeting is held, which various characters attend. These people are from all different walks of life, and they hold very different ideas and opinions. You might include:
  - councillors from the local authority;
  - the head teacher;
  - representatives of the supermarket;
  - parents of children who attend the school;
  - members of staff, for instance from the PE and science departments.
- The students work as their characters within the format of the council meeting. They must argue from this person's specific point of view, putting forward ideas and giving supporting evidence to show why the proposal should, or should not, go ahead.

- At the end of the meeting you might take a vote to see whether or not the proposal has been accepted. You could also spend some time discussing whether any of the children have changed their minds, and why.

You might choose to give out the roles beforehand, allowing time for research and discussion in preparation for the meeting. As I pointed out earlier in this section, it makes an interesting approach to ask the students to argue a position that they do not actually believe in. Alternatively, you could simply start up the meeting yourself, perhaps in the role of the head teacher, and then coax the children to join in by asking them questions. For example, you might point to a child and say *'I understand that your child is in the school football team, Mrs Jones. What do you feel about the issue of losing some of the sports facilities?'*

Just one word of warning, though: do ensure that you make it clear to the children that the whole thing is a fiction. I have heard of a case where a teacher used this exercise and subsequently had panicked phone calls from parents asking what was going on. It turned out that a copy of the letter had fallen into the hands of a student who didn't know that the exercise was imaginary.

Debates

Debates offer the teacher an excellent way of developing thinking skills, particularly in working with creating and developing arguments, and considering persuasive techniques. The old-fashioned debating format, although perfectly valid, does perhaps lack a certain something for the streetwise kids of today. In fact, debating lends itself very well to some extremely modern formats.

Why not spice up this old favourite for our children, by adapting it into a structure used on television? You could take your inspiration from a television show that features 'for' and 'against' arguments – for instance *Kilroy*. Set up the classroom in the same way as on the TV show, and start your children debating an issue or idea within the format as seen on television.

Thinking about consequences

We all wish that our children would consider the consequences of their actions more fully. This, of course, is how good behaviour management works in the classroom (and indeed in the home). We encourage our students to understand that certain misbehaviours will result in certain consequences. We also try to ensure that the consequences are the same every time a specific misbehaviour occurs. So it might be that the sanction (or consequence) for not completing work is a detention in which the work will be finished.

Consequences play a much wider role in our children's lives outside of school, as they learn and develop their social skills. Understanding about consequences becomes especially important as our students grow older, and the potential outcome of the actions they might take starts to become more serious. For instance, the teenager who decides to experiment with drugs needs to understand that there are various consequences involved: from the possibility of physical or psychological side effects, to the dangers of addiction, to the chances of getting caught and punished by the legal system.

Consequences can be short term or long term, and the potential consequences of a single action or event might be short or long lasting. For example, a short-term consequence of not completing homework might be receiving a punishment the next day in school. In the longer term, the consequences of repeatedly not doing homework could include a lack of a proper education, a student not entering university, and consequently not finding a good job.

Below are some different exercises that you can use to develop your students' awareness and understanding of the consequences of their actions.

Fictional scenarios

A useful approach for teaching your students about consequences is to give them a number of different fictional (but true to life) scenarios to think about. Ask them to consider the different actions that the character might take and what the consequences of each action could be. You might approach this exercise as a whole class discussion task, or you could get the children working in groups, perhaps even acting out their different storylines and the potential consequences. Encourage the students to think beyond the initial consequences and to look into the longer term penalties. Here is a sample scenario to show you how this would work.

Scenario
Sarah is 15 years old. She goes to a night club with her 18-year-old boyfriend, John. She is offered an Ecstasy tablet and she decides to take it.

Consequences
There are a whole variety of potential consequences that the children might suggest. Here are some examples:

- She has a great time, and really enjoys the experience. The next time she goes out clubbing she takes another tablet, and soon she is addicted.
- She hates the experience, and is violently sick. This puts her off the whole idea of taking drugs and she decides to break up with John.
- She decides to save the tablet and take it later. That evening, the club is raided by the police, and Sarah is found in possession of drugs. She is taken to the police station.

The judgement chair

The judgement chair is a drama technique for exploring characters and how they relate to each other. The format is simple but powerful. Depending on the topic you are studying, you choose one student to play a character and sit in the 'judgement chair'. The other members of the class then approach this character in various different roles. The person in the chair talks to them or with them about what that person has done, basically passing judgement on the actions of the person in the chair. The consequences of what this character has done are brought out in the responses of others. The person under judgement may choose to respond to what is said, or may simply listen to people's accusations.

Perhaps the best way to show you how this exercise works is to give you an example. Let's say you want to teach the class about bullying, and the potential harm it can do. Ask for a volunteer to play the bully – this person then goes to sit in the judgement chair. The other children then approach the bully and speak with them, choosing a character within which to talk, and making it clear who they are through what they say. Here's an extract from the scene that follows:

Child 1:	How could you treat me like that? What did I ever do to you? I hate the way you bully me. Sometimes, when I go home I spend the whole evening crying. I hate you and people like you.
Child 2:	I'm embarrassed to call you my son. I was so ashamed when the school called me and told me what you had been doing. Did I bring you up to be so cruel?
'Bully':	Don't give me that, mum. You were rubbish when I was a kid, always smacking me and shouting at me. It's your fault I'm like I am.
Child 2:	How dare you talk to me like that! Just you wait until I get you home, I'll show you who's boss.
Child 3:	I thought something was happening to Tracey. She always seemed so upset in my lessons. Now I know what you've been doing and I won't stand for it in my class. I'm going to report you to the head teacher, and she'll decide what should be done.

Flour babies

I just love this idea, and I've used it on a number of occasions, with varying results. The title 'flour babies' is taken from a book by Anne Fine, in which a teacher hands out bags of flour which the children must care for, just as though they were real babies. The exercise is designed to help the students understand the real pressures and responsibilities of being a parent. The idea is very simple – bags of flour are given out and a period of time is set for the babysitting. I have used periods of between one and two weeks. During this time, the students must take full responsibility for their 'babies' – for instance, if they have to leave the babies at any time, they must arrange for an appropriate carer to take charge.

There are a number of variations on this theme. Some teachers have used eggs instead, although I can imagine the messy results if the eggs are not hard boiled! You can now obtain computerized babies that actually keep a record of how the parent has done (you may have seen these in use on a series of *Big Brother*). However, these are expensive to buy and perhaps take a little of the fun and imagination out of the activity.

I have used this exercise with a whole range of different children. In a 'tough' school at which I worked, it was undertaken with great seriousness, to the extent of dressing the bags of flour up in knitted outfits and arranging for babysitters to cover evenings out. Surprisingly, perhaps, the activity worked least well at the 'easiest' school where I've taught. Here, I duly handed out the bags of flour to my drama class and waited to see what would happen. By morning break there were telltale explosions of flour on the playground floor, by lunchtime I had students coming to me in floods of tears, explaining how their babies had been kidnapped!

Thinking and the 'big' questions

The 'big' questions of life offer us some really meaty material for thinking work, and can lead to some great discussions within the classroom. Perhaps one of the best ways of approaching the 'big' questions is via discussion work, whether this is as a whole class or in small groups. These issues are ones that often trouble our children, and they will probably welcome the chance to hear what others have to say. Here are several points that you might like to bear in mind when approaching work on the 'big' questions.

- *Set the ground rules:* Before you start, it's a good idea to spend some time talking about beliefs and how different people might believe in different ideas. Although there is no compulsion for your children to actually change what they believe, I think it's important to insist that everyone listens to other students' points of view, giving respect and time to opinions that may vary widely from their own.
- *Give it enough time:* Discussions about such big and important ideas will inevitably take up a good amount of time, especially if we hope to explore them in sufficient detail. Often, a discussion that starts out looking at one point will lead on to various other avenues of thought, and it is a real shame to have to cut things short just as they are getting going.
- *Be sensitive:* We do need to tread very carefully when discussing moral and particularly religious ideas. For some of our children, their beliefs will form an integral part of their lives outside of school, and they may find it difficult to question the values that they hold. If you decide to lead a discussion into these areas, you will need to be very sensitive in dealing with your children's emotions.
- *Understand a limited point of view:* In some circumstances, our children's beliefs will be so strongly held that they will find it hard to entertain the possibility of other viewpoints. Again, this applies particularly to the question of religious values. Although we obviously want to encourage our students to think widely and with an open mind, we must also understand that for some this will prove a challenge to all that they have been brought up to believe.
- *Admit that you don't have all the answers:* Some of your children will be looking to you as their teacher for answers to some very difficult questions. Be willing to admit that you do not necessarily have the solutions to all the issues that trouble them. In fact, with these questions no one can give one 'true' and correct answer anyway, because so much is down to subjective, personal belief.

You can find a whole host of different questions below to guide your discussions on the big questions of life. You will also find a suggestion for an exercise to help get your children thinking about and working with moral dilemmas.

Questions about 'existence'

- 'What is a soul?'
- 'Do animals have souls?'
- 'Is there a separate spirit that exists apart from our bodies?'
- 'What do you think happens to you when you die?'
- 'Are we alone in the universe, or is there life on other planets?'
- 'Do ghosts exist?'
- 'What is happiness?'
- 'What is truth?'

Questions about morality

- 'What is right?'
- 'What is wrong?'
- 'What is good?'
- 'What is bad?'
- 'What is evil?'
- 'Are some people born evil?'
- 'Why is it wrong to steal?'
- 'If there is no such thing as "God", is there any reason why people should be good?'
- 'Is it better to be rich or to be happy?'
- 'Is it better to be good or to be happy?'

Questions about religion

- 'What or who is "God"?'
- 'Is there one right and correct religion?'
- 'Can a number of different religions all be "right"?'
- 'What do you believe happens when we die?'
- 'Is there such a thing as heaven?'
- 'What is hell like?'
- 'Is there such a thing as reincarnation?'
- 'If there is, how does it work?'

Moral dilemmas

If students explore their reactions to specific moral dilemmas, this helps make the decisions between 'right' and 'wrong' more concrete and realistic for them. As well as asking your children to discuss the moral dilemmas below, you could also ask them to act out the scenes, looking at the various different options available to them. Encourage the students to come up with as many alternatives as they can possibly find, rather than simply saying what they would do in a particular situation. Ask them to apply creative thinking to establish all the possible storylines and the likely outcomes of different moral decisions.

Scenario one. You are alone in the classroom at break time with your best friend. He asks you to help him steal money from the teacher's handbag. He says that he needs the money to buy his mother a birthday present. Do you help him? If you refuse to join in, but he steals the money anyway, what do you do?

Scenario two. You borrow your sister's favourite outfit to go to a party, but without asking her permission. While you are at the party, someone spills a drink all over the outfit, and stains it badly. What do you do? Do you tell your sister what has happened, or do you replace the outfit and hope she doesn't notice? If she does spot the stain, what are you going to say?

Scenario three. You decide to give up sweets for a month, and you persuade your family to sponsor you for Children in Need. On the last day of the month, a friend offers you a piece of chocolate, and without thinking you eat it. What do you do? Should you tell your sponsors what has happened, or keep quiet and collect the money for charity?

9

Thinking around the curriculum

In this new chapter, you'll find a whole host of interesting ideas for developing thinking skills in different areas of the curriculum, both at primary and at secondary level. These ideas have been sent to me by teachers from around the UK and beyond. You'll hear the teachers describe their approaches in their own words, and talk about how their children respond to the activities.

Many, many thanks to all the teachers who took time out of their busy schedules to send me these ideas. If you have any suggestions that you'd like to contribute to the next edition of this book, do please send them to me at sue@suecowley.co.uk.

Tracey Dunn

I regularly use 'thinking starters' where the children are challenged to think. For example, about:

- everything they know about an apple or another object;
- what I might have in my school bag;
- what they could do with a swimming hat.

I've done this with Year 3 and Year 6, so it would work for all ages. My colleague in Year 1 has done it with her children too.

I use a thinking journal, where we make time each week for the children to record what they've learnt, what they've done that has surprised them and their thoughts about our 'big questions'.

I also have a 'Can you beat the teacher?' challenge board where the children write down questions that they would like answers to and which they think I can't answer. The type of questions vary with the age group (I've done it with Years 3, 5 and 6) and it's made us think about the type of questions that we ask. For example we've had: 'How many hairs will a man grow in his beard over his lifetime?'; 'Why, when I add blue bubble bath to my bath water, are the bubbles always white?'; and 'How many blades of grass are there in the school field?' We've also done, 'Which came first, the chicken or the egg?'

I also did a thinking skills project for my MA. I set out to explore how developing children's thinking would impact on raising standards, although this changed a little with my reading. The aims became to understand children's perceptions of themselves as thinkers, and to widen children's thinking socially and intellectually by enabling them to become willing to take risks with their learning in a range of situations and to become effective problem-solvers.

It was an action research project and the data I collected was through a variety of methods including questionnaires to address the first aim. Through my general teaching I set problems that had to be solved. I built most of the problems into the geography unit of work on the local area. The problems were set and the children worked in groups to achieve a solution over a half term, planning what they were going to be doing and how they would be doing it. (This was a Year 3 class with a significant number of children on the SEN register and with behaviour problems.)

The problems included: to make a replica model of their section of Calne (following some fieldwork), to plan a village producing a plan and land-use map showing the physical and human features of the village, to include a sculpture or statue that gives a message about their village (linked to art and the sculpture that is in Calne) and to present their village plans to a planning committee. To begin the second problem I had a town planner come in and talk to the children.

How to problem-solve and work in groups was the theme of circle time along with thinking exercises. The children kept a thinking journal and were encouraged to jot down ideas between sessions to remind them of what they had done or what they wanted to do next.

The project ran over a period of six months and I did find that the children became more confident in themselves as thinkers and their self-esteem rose. A knock-on effect was their behaviour improved and they engaged more in their work. I found that they were able to work together regardless of the groups they were in – friendship or imposed – and they were able to achieve solutions. I did intervene when necessary when disputes arose but this intervention was usually to encourage them to reflect on the circle time and how they could solve the disputes for themselves.

The university has used this project as an exemplar for others so it was considered a good piece of work.

Karen Garner

Here are the poems Sue [Karen's TA] and I used. 'Yesterday mum cooked again' is the one we started with – and developed a story in a circle, each child adding an idea about what happened before/after, thinking about the consequences. It was fab because Dad ended up losing his job because he had to take Mum to hospital (again) and was late for work.

We followed this up with the one about the daughter breaking the plates – the children said Dad had taken Mum out to buy her some new dishes as a treat for her disaster in the kitchen. Again they thought about what had happened before and the consequences.

I think these poems are lovely and as they are short they were good to use in a small intervention group. Mark has created some wonderful poems that are just an amazing tool for emotional literacy. They help children to think about events and their consequences.

Yesterday mum cooked again
Yesterday mum cooked again.
The fire engine left this morning.
Dad is not happy

He must paint the kitchen again.
Today we are having fish and chips.
Dad says we need a cook
Or a new mum.
But we like the Mum we have
So if you can cook
Will you do our dinner tomorrow?

© Mark Angliss

Sometimes I go in the blue light taxi
Sometimes I go in the blue light taxi
to the place where Mum and Dad smile a lot but always look sad.
I get comics and lots of toys
and the nurses give me lots of puffers.
Soon I feel better, but I have to stay anyway,
sometimes for two or three nights . . .
I think they like me there
And don't want me to go.

© Mark Angliss

My Dad says I am like a little elephant
My dad says I am like a little elephant.
But my ears are not big
And my nose is cute as a button said mum.
I do not have four legs, just two
Just like you.
Sometimes I break things, but not because I am an elephant,
I don't even like peanuts.
I break things because my hands are small and things are so big,
Especially plates.
Why can't I have my dinner on my toy tea set?

© Mark Angliss

My dad drinks coffee
My dad drinks coffee
My mum drinks tea.
Dad is a bit fat
And mum is really thin.

Dad likes war films
And mum likes love stories and kissing.
Yuk!
I do not know why they are friends
But I love them anyway.

© Mark Angliss

Julie Elliott

I am a Year 4 teacher with curriculum responsibility for history. I am currently writing up my dissertation for my Masters and have used *Getting the Buggers to Think* and enjoyed the easy-to-read, no-nonsense and non-jargon approach.

I have recently written a series of history activities based on an historical study of Cardiff Castle. Being interested in memory and the retention of facts, I designed an activity whereby pupils had to reconstruct a puzzle of the William Burges designed clock tower at Cardiff Castle. Half the class were given the puzzle and told to reconstruct pieces to form a tower. The other half of the class were given an adaptation of the architect's instructions to the builders.

At a plenary, the design of the tower was discussed, emphasizing the points made in the original instructions. Some six weeks later all pupils were assessed as to their retention of six facts relating to the building of the clock tower. Those pupils who used the instructions to construct the puzzle were assessed as being better able to retain the six facts.

Although this activity was designed for use when studying Cardiff Castle it could be adapted for any historical building or artefact. Teachers could adapt their own list of instructions or facts.

[Activity reproduced with kind permission of Cardiff Advisory Service for Education and Cardiff Castle.]

Beth Dennis

This is a logic-based activity aimed at Key Stage 3 or 4 students. They have to fit 18 bottles into a 6 × 4 crate with the rule that

193

there must be an even number of bottles in every row and column. The solution can be achieved only if one row is full and three columns are full. This activity was introduced to me as interesting for a first lesson as you can explain this and use it to reinforce how important it is that the students listen to you. The results can then generate some interesting discussions about which arrangements are the same. This problem generates some interesting extension problems:

- How many different solutions are there?
- Is a solution possible for all different sizes of crate?
- What changes as you change the number of bottles?

Sarah-Jane Rhead

With my maths A-level class, we have an imaginary student named 'Ivor Cockedup'. Basically I complete an activity, question or equivalent but in each answer there is a deliberate mistake/assumption. The students then have to take on the role of the marker/teacher and go through correcting the work. Sometimes I tell them how many mistakes they are looking for, sometimes I don't, depending on the situation. This teaches the students to check their own work with a 'marking' hat on. They do tend to work more carefully for a period of time afterwards.

Here's another idea. The grid below was shown while students entered the room and while I took the register, with the instruction to study it. The grid was then removed and I asked the questions. This could easily be adapted with a different order, more or fewer squares, any contents and questions suitable for the group. I used this particular grid with a mixed-ability, Year 7 class.

0.1	0.2	0.3
0.4	0.5	0.6
0.7	0.8	0.9

Starter questions:
I will read each question twice. Give all of your answers to one decimal place, e.g.: Top left plus bottom right = 0.1+0.9 = 1.0

1) Total sum of the four corners = 0.1+0.3+0.7+0.9 = 2.0
2) Middle square in the bottom row − Top square of the middle column = 0.8 − 0.2 = 0.6
3) Total sum of the left-hand column = 0.1+0.4+0.7 = 1.2
4) Bottom row − left-hand column = (0.9+0.8+0.7) − (0.1+0.4+0.7) = 2.4 − 1.2 = 1.2
5) Total sum of all the squares? 4.5

Maria Selby

With my Year 7s:

1. I read the letters from the *New Scientist* book *Does Anything Eat Wasps*? The children love it and most of the time, after some discussion between themselves, they can think up an answer along the lines of the experts in the book. We have got a bit carried away in the past and done it for the whole lesson!
2. I have a selection of curious toys that I either use as a whole lesson where the children move around stations and try each one, or just use one as a starter. The idea is that the children come up with how it works or why it works. At the end, we discuss everyone's ideas or groups feedback what they think for particular toys. I find the children come up with all kinds of weird and wonderful ideas but then build on each other's ideas to get the right answer. They seem to really enjoy it too and have been overheard asking their friends what they think. I use stuff I have been given or buy cheap toys; most of these can be bought from Hawkin's Bazaar.
3. Exciting demos/toys at the start of a lesson or as a one-off lesson also get them thinking. Below is a list of the things I do at the Oxford University Natural History Museum 'Wow How?' day (science fun stuff). It's a collection of stuff gained from a number of sources . . . . Any year group (the younger they are

the more practice they need) can do them; Year 10 seems to be best.

Science fun stuff

Activity	What you need	What you do	What happens
Magnet and copper tube	Earth magnet and copper tube	Drop the magnet down the tube	Magnet drops very slowly due to the induced current *Safety: don't allow small children to have the magnet (choking hazard if swallowed)*
Air blaster	Air blaster and silver foil	Point the blaster at some silver foil	Blaster pushes air which is seen by the silver foil crumpling up *Safety: don't shoot it at people*
Magic sand	Magic sand (http://jchemed. chem.wisc.edu/ Journal/Issues/ 2000/Jan/abs40 A.html), cup and water	Stir the magic sand in the water/bring it out of the water	Magic sand is hydrophobic and therefore does not get wet *Safety: don't spill water/eat sand*
Diving ketchup	1 litre drinks bottle, water and ketchup sachet	Squeeze the bottle and watch the ketchup sink	Air in the ketchup sachet is compressed, making it more dense, so it sinks *Safety: lid on bottle = contained*
Wailing ball	Wailing ball	Touch the connections to	Connecting a cicuit

Activity	What you need	What you do	What happens
		make the ball wail	
Balloon in a bottle	2 drinks bottles, one of which has a small hole in the bottom, 2 balloons	Try to blow up a balloon inside a bottle	Can't do it because of pressure but you can in a bottle with a hole in *Safety: antiseptic wipes*
Lemonade lava lamp	Fizzy water/ lemonade, cup and sultanas	Put lemonade and sultanas in a cup and watch sultanas move up and down	Lifted by bubbles and drop when they pop *Safety: don't spill fluid*
Oil and water lava lamp	Glass of water, cooking oil and salt	Glass of water with a thick layer of cooking oil on top, pour salt on and watch	*Safety: don't spill*
Amazing marsh-mallows	Marshmallows, bottle and wine air remover	Pump air out of bottle and watch	Air pressure reduces so marshmallows expand
Magic balloon	Balloon, plastic rod and duster	Rub both balloon and rod with duster and use the rod to magically move the balloon	Balloon and rod have opposite charges so balloon follows the rod
Screaming bar	Aluminium bar	Rub fingers down bar to make it scream	Resonance
Ping-pong ball in water	Beaker of water, ping-pong ball and towel	Swill the beaker with the ping-pong ball in and watch	Ping-pong ball jumps out *Safety: warn people, don't spill the water*
Magic candles	Two candles of different sizes, plate, and large plastic container and matches	Light candles and put container over	CO_2 rises as it is hot and puts out the taller candle *Safety: care with*

Activity	What you need	What you do	What happens
			candles and matches
Tea bag burners	Tea bag, match	Light end of the tea bag and watch it float up and burn out	Tea bag completely burns up before it reaches head height *Safety: care with matches and stand back from lit tea bag*
Matches	Plate, water, coins, match and glass	Water on plate, stack of coins in middle, light match and rest on coins, put glass over top	Water puts out match *Safety: care with matches*

4. I've done a lot of concept mapping with my classes too. (I did this as a project for my PGCE+ assignment.) I've found that creating a list of key words and then photocopying these onto different coloured paper really helps as the pupils can have a different colour to the person sitting next to them and the words don't get mixed up. I give the following instructions:
   i.   Cut out the words and set aside any you don't know.
   ii. Start with two words you know – how are they connected? Stick these down on a piece of A3 and write the connection on a line connecting the two words.
   iii. Keep going with all of the words, until you've connected as many as possible.

Pupils need lots of practice at this but my classes have really caught on and are doing well at it.

Jacqueline Peace

Here's an idea I had about using role play/'ask the expert' to get students to use what they know about databases, spreadsheets and word-processing and analyse a situation ready to design a new system for a situation. It's an adaptation of an idea that the head of ICT at my school has used.

> *Teacher enters classroom (sticky plaster on his/her nose, a pair of 'L' plates and a scruffy-looking diary labelled 'Bookings').*
>
> *The teacher plays Han Brake, a driving instructor who runs his/her own driving school with two other instructors; or at least did until Miss Steer reversed into the driving school office – a proper 'system crash'. The filing cabinet has been crushed and all the neatly typed and photocopied driving lesson application forms and all the handwritten student contact details in the card filing system have been scattered and ruined by the fire sprinkling system.*
>
> *Han needs to set up the whole system again but can't face having to redo all that handwriting and typing.*
>
> *Han needs to let all the students know about the crash so they'll be more understanding if there are delays in getting them lessons until a replacement car has been sorted out. Unfortunately, the handwriting is too scrawled in the 'Bookings' book to see who needs to be contacted to cancel their lessons. Han would like to give a promotional offer so the school won't lose its customer base. Writing to all 100 students is a hefty task if done by hand! The school needs a better way to book lessons, too; the diary is too messy with crossings out – a daily lesson schedule for each driving instructor would be an excellent improvement.*
>
> *Han has been told that he/she would be better off using a computer but has never used one, so doesn't know how much they cost or what needs to be done to get the data into it and isn't convinced that it would be any quicker to find customer details and bookings.*

The idea is that the students need to think of relevant questions to ask the driving school instructor. They would then be able to *analyse* the situation and work out what *hardware and software application(s)* they would recommend and how they could start a new *computer-based system* to keep student records and booking neatly organized.

Hopefully they will have enough experience by the time they meet this exercise to be able to see the problem areas and the interview with the driving instructor will allow them to think about the issues involved, e.g. *searching and sorting* is best done with a *database application*, this could be linked by *mail-merge to word processor application, data collection forms, data input screens*, etc., etc. . . .

When I did this activity with my Year 9 class, I decided to combine your idea of a 'talking stick' with the activity and passed round one of the 'L' plates – only the people holding an 'L' plate could speak, i.e. Rhonda Bend (I didn't fancy calling myself Han Brake) and the 'Expert'.

I have to say that it worked like a dream, despite me fumbling with nerves to get the plaster stuck and my inexperience at keeping the group politely quiet. The questions, ideas and suggestions that flowed were really impressive – a real credit to my Year 9 class! I am so delighted that I'm going to repeat the exercise with my other Year 9 group, lots with SEN IEPs, so I think I might need to back up the plenary with a simple writing frame. My class commented that I am the most down-to-earth 'schitzo' they have ever come across!!!

Theresa McEvoy

The beanbag game

I ask all the students to stand in a circle and raise their right hand. I pass the beanbag to one of the students and tell them to pass it across the circle – as soon as a person receives the beanbag and passes it on they put their hand down so that everyone receives the beanbag once only. Then the students must repeat the passing pattern exactly but this time without the aid of the hands. Then I introduce a second beanbag (it helps if it is a different colour) and reveal that the pattern of passing must be repeated but *in the opposite direction*. Once they have mastered both techniques I make both beanbags go round the circle at the same time, and there are plenty of other variations that can be used. I find it is a good physical activity to get students thinking at the start of a lesson but it works best the first time when they don't know what it is that they are being asked to do!

Beat the panel

This one was introduced at an INSET in Australia and I just think it is a terrific idea. Students are given a piece of text to read. This could be part of a story, a newspaper article or textbook pages. They are given a time limit – very short – to retain as much information as possible. Three students are then chosen as 'the panel'. They sit or stand at the front of the class and are 'tested' in turn by the other students about what was in the text. If a student manages to ask a question that the chosen panelist cannot answer, they replace them as part of the panel. It is amazing how carefully kids will read the text, and how much they want to be on the panel! And the 'questioners' have to think around the subject to try and beat the panel.

Cracking the code

Again there are many variations of this activity, and it can be adapted to fit a particular subject requirement, but in its simplest format it revolves around the names of the students involved. I arrange the classroom with chairs behind me – the 'city of learning' – and students may only enter it once they have cracked the code. They must tell me what they wish to bring with them and how they are feeling. Usually I make it so that the object begins with the first letter of their first name and their 'feeling' with the last letter of their last name or a variation. They must not (openly!) communicate with each other – some students get through without knowing why, but eventually they all catch on.

Index